Verena Kast

SISYPHUS

SISYPHUS

The Old Stone – A New Way,
A Jungian Approach to Midlife Crisis

by Verena Kast

Translated and with a Foreword by
Norman M. Brown

DAIMON
VERLAG

Title of the original German edition:
Sisyphos: Der alte Stein – der neue Weg, by Verena Kast
© Kreuz Verlag AG, Zürich, 1986.

Sisyphus: The Old Stone – A New Way, A Jungian Approach to
Midlife Crisis, by Verena Kast, translated by Norman M. Brown.

Copyright © 1991 by Daimon Verlag,
Am Klosterplatz, CH-8840 Einsiedeln, Switzerland.

The translator, Norman M. Brown, Ph.D., is a therapist in
private practice and Professor of Humanities and Psychology at
Embry-Riddle Aeronautical University, Daytona Beach, Florida.

Cover by Hanspeter Kälin, photo of the author © Barbara Davatz

ISBN 3-85630-527-0

CONTENTS

TRANSLATOR'S NOTE

This book was originally published in Switzerland in 1986. As the English translation was progressing, Dr. Kast added new material to her chapter on the myth of the forty-year-old, translated here as the myth in midlife. These additions serve to sharpen the book's focus on midlife issues and the many-faceted reflection on them which the myth of Sisyphus has to offer.

It is customary in Dr. Kast's writing, as in other German works, to find the masculine pronoun used to refer to both men and women in a generic sense. Therefore I have substituted "a person" for *"man"* but continued the use of "he" and "him" where the author used it. It is clear from the gender equality in her examples and case studies that Dr. Kast applies the Sisyphus myth equally to both sexes.

FOREWORD

From Existentialism to Jungian Psychology

by Norman M. Brown

The image of Sisyphus pushing his boulder up the hill is familiar to us all. If we reached adulthood by the mid-sixties, we remember Sisyphus as the absurd hero of Albert Camus, the French Algerian novelist who was awarded the Nobel Prize for literature in 1957. But the chances are we never actually *read* Camus' book called *The Myth of Sisyphus.*

Camus' novels *The Stranger* and *The Plague* were penetrating, readable accounts of men in extreme situations. But *The Myth of Sisyphus* had only four pages about the mythical hero at the end of a difficult philosophical reflection on suicide versus engagement with a hopelessly frustrating world.

In fact, Camus' *Myth of Sisyphus* (Paris, 1942) was not translated until the two novels had made a reputation for him. And even when the translation finally came out in 1955 it was poorly received by American reviewers.[1] If Camus' poetic philosophy around the myth was easily misunderstood and soon passed by, the mythical symbol of the indefatigable hero quickly etched itself into the cultural scene. Thanks to the power of symbols, the mythical image reached much further than any of Camus' philosophical ideas, further even than any of his novels. The heroism of Sisyphus was identified with the skeptical humanist Camus himself, who for a few years in the late fifties was "guide to a generation" of youths on both sides of the Atlantic.[2]

Sisyphus was embraced by Americans as the embodiment of fruitless but courageous striving. But the French Existentialism from which the hero emerged didn't fare so well. Camus' tough-minded defiance was formed by the Nazi occupation of Europe, but America had never suffered such indignities on its own soil.

To be sure, the beatnik poets and a few playwrights like Edward Albee shocked the public with their scorn and despair. And Existentialist postulates about reality came alive in the American universities to help students cope with the crises generated when their home town religious faiths were laid low by the sciences, psychology and history.

But for the most part, Existentialism could only find a home in the mainstream of American culture by shedding most of its "gloom" and becoming more optimistic. Perhaps we did live in a meaningless world that was indifferent to our suffering. But if we could just get up the courage to *choose* a meaning or belief system for ourselves, we would get along all right.

There were those who lightened up Existentialism's gloom for American consumption. Theologian Paul Tillich thanked the Existentialists for rediscovering "the basic questions, to which Christian symbols are the answers."[3] Psychologist Erich Fromm answered the same basic questions with the all-American solution of romantic love.[4] And Viktor Frankl[5] found a will to meaning which could be satisfied by work. These were valuable intellectual responses to the challenge of Existentialism. But on the popular level, Existentialism was tamed by the brawny, anti-intellectual optimism of the American Dream.

As children, many of us were taught to "hitch our wagons to a star." In school we learned to believe in constant progress. This optimistic myth is often translated into a personal plan to climb the ladder of success and wealth for one's entire life. Pop psychology even abolishes society and the world as limitations to our dreaming by asserting that "we create our own reality" and teaching us daily affirmations to manufacture just what we need.

But the titanic urge of the American Dream is an immoderate ambition that sets us up for the frustrations of Sisyphus. By denying the existential limitations set by physical, historical, social and psychological realities, the popular mind-set both covers up and creates an awesome abyss. When the limitations caused by aging and the choices we have made in life come home to roost in midlife, that abyss opens up beneath us. We discover then that we can no longer walk on air as we could in our dreams.

In the midlife crisis we discover that we do need to reckon with our limitations after all. For pursuing our dreams has led us to live the life of Sisyphus. This is where Verena Kast's book can come to our aid.

Dr. Kast's work is not a *re*interpretation of Camus' myth of Sisyphus, because Camus never offered a full-fledged interpretation in the first place. Camus only interpreted Sisyphus' punishment, without even mentioning what the hero did to deserve it. Dr. Kast explains and interprets all of Sisyphus' deeds, so we get a much more complete basis for understanding the myth.

If midlife is the time for a reckoning between our dreams and reality, then the Existentialism represented by Sisyphus has valuable insights to offer. Dr. Kast presents here a critical reappraisal of Camus' hero. As a European accustomed to limitations of territory, she lacks the luxurious American fantasy of unlimited growth and possibilities. Therefore she takes the Sisyphean challenge to mean the discrimination between the limits of growth and the possibilities of change, and between hope and hopelessness. But as the soul of Europe emerges from the shadows of recurrent world wars, she presents us with a more purposeful philosophy than Existentialism. Dr. Kast relates the trials of Sisyphus to a coherent conception of the human life cycle in a meaningful cosmos.

The psychology of Carl Gustav Jung grew up at the same time as the Existentialism of Heidegger and Sartre, but it differs in some fundamental assumptions. Existentialism takes its name from a central tenet that existence precedes essence. That means that there is no inherent essence of human nature, so we are free to define ourselves through our choices in life. Yet this awesome responsibility for our actions cannot keep us from being thrown about or crushed by physical, social, historical and psychological forces beyond our control. In contrast, Jung found an essential human nature that precedes the choices we make in life. Human nature is not infinitely variable, so we are not able to create whatever "reality" or self we want. But neither are we completely at the mercy of external forces. Jung saw an inherent pattern unfolding in the course of each person's life that is actually the manifestation of inborn structures in the mind.

Existentialism declared we are responsible for the consequences of our choices, including their effects on others. Jung added that we were also responsible for the effects of our choices and attitudes on ourselves: We may bring on psychological suffering if we violate the hidden pattern of our own natures. On the other hand, Jung said our most basic psychological problems also derive from our intrinsic natures. Therefore our problems cannot be eliminated, only coped with, like the stone of Sisyphus.[6]

Jung agreed with the Existentialists and modern science that there is no way to verify the presence of a god in the external world. But from the universality of religions Jung concluded that the psychic structures for imaging a god are present in everyone. Thus if Sisyphus was challenging the gods in ancient Greece, he was violating the divine patterning in human nature. Sisyphus' crime and punishment can then provide clues to the secrets of human nature and development which can address issues for us all.

We should not expect a single unified interpretation of the Sisyphus myth from Dr. Kast. For Jungian analysis of myths is not a historical, anthropological or literary science with strict criteria of validity. The author uses these other disciplines as tools in a Jungian amplification of the events arranged in the myth. She interprets European folk tales, everyday incidents, attitudes and issues encountered in psychotherapy in light of the Sisyphus themes. As a result, the myth of Sisyphus becomes a kaleidoscope through which we can look deeply into our own lives and gain a little wisdom from each facet.

This book does more than just explain the value for our lives of the Greek wisdom embodied in the myth. As a Jungian analyst, Dr. Kast has mined her own experiences and those of contemporaries and patients to show ways in which we can see ourselves reflected in the myth.

Few of us will be entirely comfortable identifying with Sisyphus' fate. But when our individual or collective American Dreams crash before our eyes, we can learn to face the disappointment and the void without collapsing, escaping into intoxicants or complaining like the cynic. We can cease our Sisyphean labors or choose to take up our stone again, realizing *this* time that the path we follow *is* the goal.

Norman M. Brown

Notes:

1. "It is all very high powered and confusing…" *The New Yorker*, April 14, 1956, 174. "Camus has an 'interesting' mind, one that momentarily attracts because of its penchant for expressing epigrammatically lucid reasons for holding improbable beliefs." *Yale Review*, Spring 1956, 46. The most popular magazine was the most snide, concluding: "Most will agree with Camus that the disappearance of God from the calculations of the modern intellectual has put a rope of despair around his neck. And they may respect Camus' astonishingly simple faith that things will be more comfortable if it is agreed to call despair 'lack of hope,' and the rope a cravat." *Time*, Oct. 3, 1955, 100. Even William Barrett, whose book *Irrational Man* collected and introduced basic Existentialist writings for Americans, was unenthusiastic about the philosophy of Sisyphus: "It is a difficult ideal of life, and maybe too narrow and thwarting a one; but it is also one that one cannot help but admire." *Saturday Review*, Oct. 8, 1955, 14.

2. Thomas Molnar, then a professor at Brooklyn College, opens his article, "A. Camus: Guide of a Generation," this way: "Nine students out of ten, if asked to name a contemporary author with the greatest impact on youth, will mention Albert Camus in the first place." *Catholic World*, Jan. 1958, 186:272.

3. Tillich, Paul, first published in *Christianity and the Existentialists*, ed. Carl Michalson, reviewed and quoted in *Time*, July 16, 1956, 87.

4. "Love," says Dr. Fromm, "is the only satisfactory answer to the problem of human existence." Quoted on the frontispiece of the Bantam paperback edition of Fromm, Erich, *The Art of Loving*, first published New York, Harper & Row, 1956.

5. Frankl, Viktor, *Man's Search for Meaning: An Introduction to Logotherapy*. Boston, Beacon Press, 1959.

6. American psychotherapy seems to be invested in denying and disproving the limitations to its efficacy which both Freudians and Jungians have accepted as a fact. From hypnosis to drugs and cognitive behaviorism to body work, numerous American therapies have soared and fallen from favor on the presumption that complete and lasting cures are possible. On the popular front, Rolfing, Rebirthing and Scientology have also made the same immoderate claims of cures. But Alcoholics Anonymous is more modest, like Jung, from whom its founder, Bill W., received encouragement and support.

INTRODUCTION

One day as I was busily clearing away a mountain of dishes it occurred to me how soon there would be another mountain of dishes to take its place. I began to imagine how many more mountains of dishes would follow this one in the course of my life and how many I have already carried away. This is a task that repeats itself with monotonous uniformity and is never accomplished for more than a moment, a task that will continue to repeat itself. My eternal dishwashing, it seemed true to me, is a labor of Sisyphus.

Upon further contemplation I became aware that for as long as I could remember the radio news reports have had a similar ring. The world problems continue to be discussed and debated without anything substantial ever changing. Even more monotonous than that is the format of reporting which always remains the same: Much room is always given to the tragedies in the world while little attention is paid to happy events.

I could see a connection between my kitchen task, eternally repeating itself and never completely finished, and the problems of humanity, which are constantly confronted yet always recurring. Of course I could turn my attention to the satisfaction that comes at the moment when the mound of dishes has been cleared away, and I could concentrate on the tiny improvements that can be discerned in the repetitious news reports. But on this particular day I was struck by the vision of eternal repetition. It was suddenly clear to me that there are an infinite number of things in life that are forever starting over, and that I'm always having to start from square one myself, particularly in those matters in which a change would be more than welcome.

Other experiences came to mind that correspond to this theme: The many times I have tried to explain the same piece of subject matter; my habit of approaching a problem from every conceivable angle until I think that I have figured it out, only to conclude later that I haven't yet defined it succinctly enough. So I turn it over in my mind once again, reformulate and describe it anew. Here too I keep starting from the beginning.

It was evident that dishwashing should be classed as a labor of Sisyphus. But the case of humanity's struggle with its problems, as expressed in the news, was somewhat less clear cut. Even less certain was the judgment of my explanations. Of course the questions asked may be strikingly similar, but the situations that give rise to them are often different, for something has changed. My personal struggle for a vivid expression or a fitting image also involves endless repetition, and the hope of only provisional success. But despite its connection with much that is "Sisyphean" I would not consider my expressive work simply a labor of Sisyphus, for much is in constant flux.

Then I began to think about people involved in a therapeutic process. There, too, one struggles constantly with the same basic problems. The same questions arise again and again, and the same peculiarities develop into conflicts. Many a client complains, "Will I never be able to overcome this problem?" and all but gives up his efforts in despair. On other occasions, however, and from another vantage point he realizes that though he continues to be occupied with the same problems, he can deal with them in a different way. When he first despairs the client is convinced that the work on his fundamental problems is nothing more than a labor of Sisyphus. Later consideration renders him much less certain.

This gives rise to the question: Does the Sisyphean experience lose its sense of toil when one succeeds in experiencing not only the repetition, but also the subtle changes? Or, do we use the label 'a labor of Sisyphus' at those times when we are either unable or unwilling to acknowledge change?

Clearly it is difficult to see anything meaningful in those labors of Sisyphus that involve nothing but repetition. For what is meaningful is the variation we can perceive by connecting them to a more inclusive frame of reference.

ROLLING THE STONE

The mundane experience with endless dishwashing was an opportunity to make the connection between a basic attitude and a mythical image. My resistance to the eternal repetition was placed in a wider context by the identification with a mythological figure. I experienced the fundamental existential awareness of the person who appears to toil in vain.

Myths are stories constructed from the elements of everyday reality and they take the experience of this reality as their subject matter. They use this to express humankind's self-knowledge, its experience of divinity and its attitude toward both the divine and the mundane. For a myth to endure, both the collective and the individual must be able to identify with it. Thus it must express an essential human condition or yearning.

Myths have been deprived of their power by the science of history. It is clear therefore that a myth that still carries a message to us today must have a symbolic function. It must illuminate some fundamental life experiences. Each myth expresses specific fears and hopes. In the myth of Sisyphus the experience is that of a person who appears to toil in vain, yet will not be torn away from his efforts. I say appears because the phrase "in vain" implies from the outset interpretation of the myth.

Sisyphus ought to "succeed": he should roll the stone over the peak and put an end to the business. But should he really? Don't we tend to call a task a labor of Sisyphus, or label efforts as Sisyphean, in those very situations where we are convinced that a goal must be reached?

Homer has Odysseus tell of his journey through the underworld:

> Then Sisyphus in torment I beheld
> being roustabout to a tremendous boulder.
> Leaning with both arms braced and legs driving,
> he heaved it toward a height, and almost over,
> but then a Power spun him round and sent
> the cruel boulder bounding again to the plain.
> Whereon the man bent down again to toil,
> dripping sweat, and the dust rose overhead.[1]

This well known part of the myth conveys great exertion, intense engagement and perseverance with the boulder, even though the supposed goal cannot be reached. This is followed by endless repetition, which according to the myth is a punishment from the gods.

Like all myths that still affect us, the myth of Sisyphus expresses a fundamental experience of human existence, an essential aspect of life and human nature.

THE EVERYDAY APPRECIATION OF THE MYTH

The fact that the power of this myth has survived was reflected in the reactions of my acquaintances when I told them that I was currently exploring the myth of Sisyphus. The news met with a sigh or a laugh of understanding, of bitterness and occasionally of malice. All of them showed that this theme was not foreign to them. Conversations developed around the theme of resignation, the will to persevere and the meaning and absurdity of existence. Feelings of being overwhelmed were expressed, along with the conviction that the time would come when one would be unable or unwilling to lift this eternal stone any longer. Questions were raised which brought the issue of hope and hopelessness to the fore. In connection with the life situation of each individual other aspects of this significant mythical image were given more attention. For some people the most significant aspect was that of exertion against the heavy stone viewed as a symbol for a difficult task causing suffering. For others it was the eternal repetition which they experienced as painful. It was the endless repetition that made the "stone" heavy. In the final analysis, however, most of the people agreed that the burden and the repetition combine to cause the suffering.

There were other reactions, however. There were people who felt that the repetition did them good, for it was the expression of an order on which one could depend. They accepted that which was always the same, because they understood it to be an expression of the essence of life. Although some felt deprived of innovation in this model of life, others were pleased that for once novelty was not all important.

It soon became clear from the reactions to the myth that different aspects of it can be experienced, and that these reactions are heavily dependent upon the role the myth plays in the current life situation of each individual. For it goes without saying that not all of human existence is expressed in the myth of Sisyphus. A multitude of myths exists. All have vital things to say about the human condition, and each illuminates a different perspective. To name but one example, in contrast to the myth of Sisyphus is the myth of the holy child, which address the human ability to create and discover. The myth of Sisyphus cannot reflect the entire human condition.

It is remarkable nevertheless that this mythological motif is familiar to so many, above all because the author's native language, German, contains the expression *Sisyphosarbeit,* "Sisyphus work." As we shall see, one's stage in life shifts certain aspects of this myth into the foreground and allows others to recede.

"WHAT ENTERS YOUR HEAD WHEN YOU HEAR THE NAME SISYPHUS?"

Associations

A nineteen-year-old woman: "Labor of Sisyphus? Useless work, work from which no one gains. Pure frustration. To be avoided whenever possible."

A twenty-two-year-old man: "Labor of Sisyphus? Work that is strenuous yet accomplishes nothing. That may well be true of all work. I consider Sisyphus labor only justified when the work process as a whole contributes something, when one is able to create something in the end."

A forty-year-old woman: "Labor of Sisyphus! What strikes me about it is not so much its uselessness, but its endless repetition. Take for instance the entire job of housekeeping, the washing – there is no end to it. But of course it is necessary. Or think of the repetition of the same problems in relationships, the same arguments over the same problems, and the temptation to resolve them in the same unproductive way. Sometimes I would like to do everything quite differently."

A forty-two-year-old man: "The man who always rolled the same boulder: that's how I think of myself too. A lot that used to be challenging isn't any more. The hardship remains, but the feeling of triumph is gone. The challenge seems to be to bear this deficiency, and I'm already resigning myself to it. I have no more energy left. It's no big deal. Most people have their own stone to roll. I used to be admired for my perseverance. Now it's just become natural. Sometimes I'm even criticized for it."

A seventy-five-year-old woman: "Labor of Sisyphus. I haven't thought about that in a long time. Earlier, when I was in my forties, there was so much to do and I seemed constantly to be starting from scratch again. I only have to think of the mountains of socks that always needed mending, and of how they were constantly holed again. It seemed so senseless. Often I was so angry I cried. Nowadays I have much less work, at least that's how it appears. One day I probably just accepted it all. After all, there is another side to it: If things are bound to get dirty again, then there's no need to clean them as if in preparation for eternal life. That's just the way things are. Everything repeats itself – and that too is good. It gives one a sense of being on intimate terms with life. One has strategies for dealing with it. One does things a little differently each time. And somehow I was always proud of the way I coped.

Today I notice the problem far more internally than externally. For I have qualities that have always made my life difficult, and they continue to make it hard. I'm sure that I have been consciously struggling with these problems for close to thirty years: Time and again this endless father complex. I know that things can't be any different, but I don't give up the struggle."

A seventy-three-year-old man: "I was a teacher. To this day I wonder where I got the strength to keep teaching the pupils the same thing over and over again. There were always the same problems encountered and the same questions asked. Sometimes I thought it was really Sisyphus work when I was discouraged, when I had the feeling that the pupils weren't learning what was essential. But of course that's not true. I was only reminded of Sisyphus when I was discouraged or when I expected too much.

Now I think of Sisyphus in connection with death in the sense that I have been pushing the boulder for an entire lifetime. I didn't run away. After all, I could have put the stone down and left. Now I really don't know if what I did was right or not."

When we compare these statements, we are struck by the fact that all of them speak of Sisyphus in connection with work. The myth of Sisyphus is a myth we perceive in the context of the working person, perhaps in essence a myth of work. This view is reinforced by the fact that we are familiar with the linguistic expression "Sisyphus work," which from the outset implies a specific interpretation of the myth.

It also becomes clear that the theme of Sisyphus presents itself above all in midlife. It is then that the experience becomes existential and its issues can no longer be as easily avoided as was the case at a younger age. Of course younger people experience the theme of Sisyphus work, and they too connect it with frustration, but with a frustration that is avoidable. For people in midlife Sisyphus work no longer appears avoidable. It is considered "necessary."

And yet this necessity is most closely linked with a lack of productivity. What is necessary need not be unproductive. What presents itself here as necessary repetition obliges us to ask whether or not there is a point to it all. We sense that what is believed necessary could prove false in the final analysis. Perhaps this fear is simply a result of the tension that arises between the knowledge that not everything can be productive and an internalized demand that everything must be productive. The necessity of repetition seems to be accepted, and yet it stands in opposition to the demand that life must change. This is the tension at the heart of the myth of Sisyphus. It prompts us to consider each time whether the repetition really is necessary or whether it is just an attempt to resolve something in an unproductive way.

The forty-year-old woman speaks of Sisyphus in the

context of relationships. So it is not only external work that is viewed as repetitive but also our behavior in relationships. The same "idiosyncrasies" that change so little lead time and again to the same suffering with one another. They always engender the same form of conflict, which leads nowhere because everyone knows from the outset how it will turn out. It's "the same old tune," and no one seems capable of bringing about the slightest change to it.

Unproductive is probably the right expression in this case, since we know very well how our partner really ought to be. The behavior is also unproductive in the sense that we have become used to these repeat performances, perhaps in several partnerships already. We are no longer frightened or even alarmed.

Finally we must ask ourselves if we are keeping our involvement with the same problem in the right perspective. After all, Sisyphus is only *one* myth among many. In which cases could this perseverance be just senseless repetition?

The forty-two-year-old man experiences a completely different aspect of the myth. His associations make clear why the Sisyphus story could be classed as a myth of the forty-year-old:

By the time one is forty a lot has been learned about mastering life, external life, and the knowledge is being applied. When for the first time we master something which we assumed was beyond our abilities we are filled with a good feeling about life. Unfortunately, this feeling is unique and cannot be repeated. The best we can hope for is a good memory of it, but usually the achievement becomes unremarkable. We have grown accustomed to it ourselves, and so have those around us. This man in his forties cannot get used to the "norm," perhaps in part because he devotes all of his energy to his work and has none left for anything else. Do we have a man here for whom this myth alone explains his entire life? Is his life dominated by the Sisyphus theme? Did he perhaps learn somewhere that by loyal pushing of the stone peaks are actually attained?

It is becoming increasingly clear that the theme of Sisyphus must occupy only one place among others in our lives.

An additional phenomenon shows up here, which while related only indirectly to the myth of Sisyphus can nevertheless greatly intensify Sisyphean suffering. Admiration is much easier to come by in youth and young adulthood than later. Later there is much that simply repeats itself, much becomes "usual," even expected. If a person can't find self-worth in the loyal fulfillment of nonspectacular tasks, if he has difficulty with the ordinary, then the Sisyphus theme will prove even more torturous than it might otherwise.

My thesis that the Sisyphus theme belongs to the forty-year-olds is supported by the statement of the seventy-five-year-old woman. She reminisces about her years between the ages of forty and fifty. In her case we clearly see the senselessness which she experienced when faced with socks that were always full of holes. We see her rage in the face of a task that could never be completed.

In the end, she simply accepted the situation as an aspect of "finite life," as an expression of the fact that much of human activity is just not meant for eternity. She arrives at a sense of human moderation. Her exertion is no longer devalued just because it yields nothing absolute, and the endless duplication of effort is accepted. In the eternal repetition she perceives that she is on intimate terms with life. After all, we review learning material repeatedly in order to imprint it on our memories. Through repetition life also imprints itself on us, if we are not constantly confronted with new and unpredictable situations.

The story this woman tells shows clearly that there is a

phase of life in which the theme of Sisyphus dominates, and that this phase can be outgrown. At first she suffered and rebelled against it, but eventually accepted it as one of life's fundamental patterns. By virtue of this acceptance aspirations were relativized, and the positive aspect of repetitiveness could be experienced, namely the sense of security which it brings. The older woman shows, too, how she satisfies the need for variation, which after all exists in all of us: Though the tasks were always similar, each time she approached them slightly differently inventing new strategies. And she was proud of this. She fully developed the freedom which remained available within the limits of the situations. The small variations which are possible can take the place of grand and impossible designs if the persistence of repetition is accepted.

But the Sisyphus theme can raise its head elsewhere. At first the seventy-two-year-old viewed the mastery of external life as Sisyphus work, forever starting again from the beginning and never really coming to any end. But later she moved on to speak about "inner problems," about idiosyncrasies that have always made life difficult for her and continue to do so. In this instance it is the ability to carry on with her idiosyncrasies and to tolerate them, to be able to put up with the difficult sides of herself, which she considers Sisyphus work.

The seventy-three-year-old man brings a similar perspective to our topic when he states that he now perceives the theme of Sisyphus in conjunction with death. The gentleman identifies himself to a certain extent with Sisyphus, as a man who has spent an entire life pushing the stone. He has always tackled the tasks which have presented themselves to him, always shouldered the hardships of life and never fled. But now he has doubts about the wisdom of his conduct.

For this individual, "pushing the stone" meant fulfilling his duty. Today he feels that sometimes he could have let the stone rest in peace. If we take his statement more radically, the stone could symbolize not just duty, but all the hardship of this man's existence. Then giving up the stone would mean giving up his life, capitulating. That was something which it never occurred to him to do.

This former teacher reminisced about his professional experience in a way that shows he was able to distance himself from complete identification with the myth. Teaching entailed much repetition and called for great versatility to make that repetition palatable. The essential factor for this teacher was however not the repetition of the material. What was essential was the pedagogical passion, the unfaltering will to show something to each new group of pupils, even though it remained the same old subject for the teacher. The necessity of repeating the same material challenged him to be creative within that repetition. Repetition is only a structural element within an existence which holds the awareness of mortality. The truly essential thing is that which is illuminated within this repetition. The teacher's exertion became a labor of Sisyphus only when he was discouraged or when he hoped for too much.

From the case above we can see that Sisyphus work is not necessarily Sisyphean from the start, but that it can *become* Sisyphus work when the going gets especially tough. This may be because our expectations are too high, or because we overreach ourselves, as perhaps the teacher has done. It is too much to continuously expect of ourselves that we be at work with a pedagogical passion and remain constantly inspired within our repetition. After all, not even Sisyphus *propelled* the boulder downhill. He just let it roll! In the case of this teacher, however, one has the impression that he was all for the pushing of the stone. It is only with hindsight that he thinks he should have allowed himself a greater degree of freedom.

The associations of people in different age brackets

have given us access to the experiential perspectives which they bring to this myth. The Sisyphus tale seems to have a lot to do with the burden of mastering everyday reality. In our human interactions we bear the burden of constantly recurring behavior which can damage a relationship. In the course of living together we become a burden for each other, and we proceed to bear these burdens together. The burden can also be seen as the effort of enduring the troublesome side of our own nature.

In all of the statements it is clear that life exists in relationship to the structural element of repetition. And yet this principle of repetition is questioned suspiciously as to whether it really is necessary or whether it merely arises from our fear of change. This repetition has much in common with ordinary life, with the experience that we cannot constantly climb the highest peaks, that "peak experiences" are not a constant part of the human condition. Of course repetitions increase the older people get, because repetition is a function of time. It appears that people in midlife are significantly less capable of dealing with this than older people are. For forty-year-olds the beginning of perceptible aging is painful because so much repeats itself and so often this repetition involves starting over from the beginning. This experience of the Sisyphean always involves the question of meaning.

Certain work seems to become Sisyphus work when we want too much, when we are too strongly committed to the absolute and incapable of accepting the finite nature of our existence. In the dynamics of great expectations which are followed by disappointments we experience the tortures of Sisyphus.

REFLECTIONS ON THE MYTHICAL IMAGE

> Then Sisyphus in torment I beheld
> being roustabout to a tremendous boulder.
> Leaning with both arms braced and legs driving,
> he heaved it toward a height, and almost over,
> but then a Power spun him round and sent
> the shameless boulder bounding again to the plain.
> Whereon the man bent down again to toil,
> dripping sweat, and the dust rose overhead.[2]

It is easy to imagine this series of events. My first impression is of "rockiness." The predominating image is that of supreme exertion in the effort to impose human will on this rock. Exertion, the necessity of letting go, and the determination with which Sisyphus takes up the stone over and over again form the essentials in Homer's text. Sisyphus has to push with both hands and feet, his body drips with sweat, and a cloud of dust encircles his head.

This is an image of the greatest concentration and presence. Thus Sisyphus cannot pay attention to anything else: The stone and his exertion demand everything from him.

Sisyphus would have had to be intensely aware of himself in this situation. We too are intensely aware of ourselves when we are fully concentrated upon a task and feel at one with it. At such times we are apt to have an experience of power and of self which takes place entirely inside, because we are no longer looking at ourselves from the outside. These are the moments when we can surpass ourselves. Such moments with oneself and of oneself provide an experience of selfhood which can only come through self-abandonment.

Sisyphus has no onlookers. This part of the myth has nothing to do with the admiration of others. It is not a narcissistic demonstration of power in the sense of "take a look at this ..." It is a struggle that must be undertaken alone.

Shortly before he reaches the goal a "power" forces the boulder downward, and the hope that arose within his concentrated engagement is dashed. Within reach of the goal, at the commonest and most frustrating point Sisyphus fails. Did he imagine too soon that he had reached his goal and lose concentration as we mortals so often do?

Or was it perhaps never his intention to actually reach the goal with the boulder, but just to push it up as far as possible? Could it be that he was more intent on merely being engaged in the process than on the attainment of the perceived goal?

We know that the boulder will never reach its goal – at least within the myth. In considering this we are forced to confront our own fear that our efforts will fail in the end, that everything could prove useless, senseless, absurd, in vain. It is that thought that forces us to look for a meaning in this apparently senseless myth.

It is peculiar that the text transmits no reaction from Sisyphus when the boulder once again rolls down into the fields below. The stone is referred to as "shameless," perhaps even "shameful." With consternation one asks of what the stone ought to be ashamed. Could it be its overwhelming "power?" From Sisyphus we hear nothing at all.

What happens in the moment when the boulder rolls down into the fields? I imagine that Sisyphus jumps to one side, breathing heavily, stands still to catch his breath and then strides down again into the valley.

Agitated? Pensive? Unburdened? Would he then have eyes for the surroundings? After being so exclusively focused on the boulder and the slope, does Sisyphus then enter into a relationship with the landscape? Homer tells us nothing of this. The phase of being unburdened is not important. What counts is the phase of being burdened and the fact that he continues to accept the burden. When we work on this myth ourselves, however, we are free to look at it in a different way to those who wrote it down.

Homer speaks of a rock which Sisyphus probably has to push up a mountain, since he speaks of a peak. On antique vases which portray interpretations of the myth of Sisyphus this rock is sometimes depicted as round like a ball and sometimes as a block of stone. The size of the blocks or crags are always exaggerated in relation to Sisyphus, in order to make it seem a miracle that a human could lift such a block at all.

In nature boulders are simply there. If they are to be moved, then it must be from the outside. Since they oppose our intentions with their hardness, solidity, angularity and weight, it is generally difficult to get a boulder to move, let alone roll. Yet Sisyphus gets the boulder to move, and even to roll, repeatedly. The only goal the myth suggests he doesn't achieve with his stone is the peak.

Focusing on Sisyphus' success at moving the stone provides a perspective that could lead us to discover another meaning in the myth. We are driven to seek such an interpretation because it is uncomfortable for us to see nothing but the senseless monotony of having to start from the beginning again and again. It is precisely the painfulness of this situation that opens up our eyes to dimensions of the myth that are not openly being addressed.

Nevertheless, the myth deals first of all with failure,

though Sisyphus does not give up. Sisyphus is not allowed to give up and he is not able to give up. He renews his attempts repeatedly, resuming the effort. Is he stubborn, compulsive or hopeful? Is he full of self-confidence or of defiance? Is he a symbol of the obstinacy with which people strive to succeed in spite of the apparent hopelessness of their goals? Is he a symbol for the fact that in spite of all of our tenacity our intentions and wishes never exist in realistic relation to our ability to realize them? Is Sisyphus a model for humanity in its excessiveness, when it lacks moderation and strives to reach beyond reasonable limits?

In this regard let us look at a text from Johann Wolfgang von Goethe's "Maxims and Reflections."

> Yet the most wondrous error is one that concerns ourselves and our abilities. It is that we dedicate ourselves to a worthy task, a noble undertaking, that is beyond our abilities. We strive for a goal that we can never attain. The Tantalus-like or Sisyphus-like suffering that one feels as a result of this effort is all the more bitter, the more earnest one's intentions have been. And yet often just when we view ourselves as severed from our original intentions forever, we find something else desirable along the way, something appropriate to us with which it was actually our lot to be contented. [3]

For Goethe it is clearly immoderate ambition, the overestimation of oneself that makes us experience "Tantalus-like or Sisyphus-like suffering." It is interesting that he speaks of Tantalus and Sisyphus together. Tantalus, Sisyphus and Prometheus are the well-known penitents of the underworld. Tantalus tested the omniscience of the gods by placing his own son before them as a meal. As a punishment he must endure eternal hunger and thirst in the underworld. Above him is a tree full of fruits, but it withdraws from him when he reaches out for the branches. Beneath him is a lake, but it too recedes when he tries to draw water from it. He must suffer hunger and thirst forever, as Sisyphus must exert himself forever. Tantalus, Sisyphus and Prometheus* all competed with the gods, tried to prove themselves superior to the gods and were punished for it.

Perhaps the myth of Sisyphus is also a symbol for the fact that in spite of all our efforts nothing can really be brought to an end in human life, nothing can ever be completed. It is an intrinsic aspect of life that everything continues as long as we live.

If the myth tells us that no matter how much humans exert themselves, ultimately they will never attain their goals, then one can ask why Sisyphus doesn't just give up. The myth answers that it is part of his punishment that he cannot give up.

First Example:
The Examination

A man who is no longer young is determined to pass an examination in a discipline that probably isn't very well suited to him. He torments and tortures himself. Sometimes he gets sick before the examination is to be held. Twice already he has failed it, and he is allowed to take it a third time. He is overstretching himself, but cannot bring himself to acknowledge this. Like Sisyphus he begins anew with great tenacity.

The man appears to others to be quite set on the idea of passing the examination. Nothing else, not even the subject matter seems to interest him. Passing the test is all that counts. The fellow seems stubborn, compulsive in the

---

*Prometheus stole fire from the gods and gave it to the humans. For this he was chained to a rock to have his liver eaten all day by an eagle, only to have it grow back each night.

extreme. When he fails the test he blames the stupidity of all those who examined his paper. Two days later he brings out all his supporting documents. He wants to show everyone that he could have passed and that he has been treated unjustly. This fellow just doesn't want to give up. And he probably can't give up without losing his self-image and falling into a deep crisis of self-esteem.

Second Example:
The Picture

A painter wants to paint a picture that she sees before her inner eye, an image that is very important to her. She paints. The resulting work has great expressive power, but it does not match the artist's inner image. She tries again, painting another, and yet another picture. To the observer the woman's actions seem obsessive. She is possessed by the idea that she can take the radiance of this inner image and portray it in an external form. The painter suffers from her inability to do so. She even becomes physically sick, but continues to paint. The woman's suffering precludes the ability to do anything else, as she keeps hoping for the right moment to realize her creative vision. It is as if she were possessed by a creative demon. The artist has the energy to stick with the theme and begin again, because she clings to the hope that she will succeed. And she possesses an enormous drive to give form to no other image than the one she has pictured within. She is seized by this passion, just as the student is seized by the idea of passing the exam.

And yet there is a perceptible difference. If I characterized the student's will to persevere as stubborn, I would never view the painter's will in the same way. In the artist's case there is still hope for change. This is hardly true of the student. Though the journey he has made in the course of all his attempts has been burdened with toil and has caused him pain, he cannot draw any enrichment from what he has learned. For the painter, on the other hand, though every picture she renders fails to be the ultimate expression of what she really wants to paint, it does express something. She learns something from each picture and articulates it when she says, "I'm making great progress with my expression. Every picture teaches me something. But I'm still not successful in painting *the* picture."

To return to Sisyphus: Is he a model for the person who cannot and will not let go of a goal once he has chosen it, appearing to us as rigid and stubborn? Does the process mean nothing to him and the goal everything? Is that why he never reaches it? As observers, can we rule out the possibility that he has hope? Or does he stand as a contrasting model to the person who is seized by an idea and seeks to express it? Does he consistently and with great persistence stick to the task and keep the process at least as much in view as the goal? And should we at least attest to his right to a "justified hope?"

The difference may appear small, but it is in fact very great. In the student's case the boulder which he has shouldered is really too large. In the painter's case the boulder could also be too large. But by constantly applying herself to the task she grows with her boulder and thus her art experiences growth too. And though it may look as if she is repeating the same task, something does in fact change with each new attempt. If we express this with the mythological images, both the boulder and the path she takes with it, as well as the path the boulder takes when it rolls back down have changed. Though this change may be imperceptible from one occasion to the next, it can certainly be discerned if one looks at attempts that are separated by a matter of weeks or months.

If we can consider the boulder of Sisyphus to be a real

stone, then of course it too would change over time, it would be worn down. It is possible that due to its altered shape and momentum it would take other paths upon rolling back down.

The two people in my examples have one thing in common: They cannot free themselves from their burdens. They have to hoist their boulders, and this effort requires all the strength that they have. Neither of them have the freedom to separate themselves from their tasks. Both however experience their situations not as senseless but as having some meaning.

Viewed from the outside, however, it appears that one of the attempts was meaningless, stubborn and therefore better broken off, while the other was meaningful. This judgment is closely bound up with whether we attribute hope or hopelessness to the situation. It is also connected to the question of whether the concerted effort is simply focused on a goal or includes the experiences along the way, and whether or not a certain hope of change exists.

HOPE AND HOPELESSNESS
OR
EXPECTATION AND DISAPPOINTMENT

The second part of the Sisyphus myth has always given rise to reflections about hope and hopelessness. The best known of these are Albert Camus' in his book, *The Myth of Sisyphus.* For Camus Sisyphus is a tragic and absurd hero. Sisyphus knows that pushing the stone is a punishment from the gods, and he knows that he will not meet with success. He has no hope of mercy or of a god's intervention. Sisyphus has neither hope nor illusion, yet continues to push the stone. By so doing Sisyphus takes his fate into his own hands and thus refuses to be defeated by the gods. Being without either hope or illusion is existing without a future. According to Camus, Sisyphus lives simply in the here and now, with no anticipation of a reward. He has the "silent joy" of knowing that his fate belongs to him alone: "His rock is his own affair." [4]

Let's follow Camus' argument for a moment. Behind the hero's mighty efforts lies no hidden meaning to reward him, no better future to be earned through his work. All of that is an illusion. In spite of this Sisyphus does not flee. Significant parts of Camus' book deal with the question of whether or not one should commit suicide in the face of the absurdity of life. To flee would mean suicide, but Sisyphus does not flee, he continues to push his stone.

This is the measure of his dignity, that he neither gives up nor flees, but stays and takes responsibility for his own situation. He doesn't seek to make any god responsible for his fate, but just looks to himself. Sisyphus takes responsibility for that part of his situation which is within his own power. This attitude is central to Existentialism. It is also anticipated in the motto which Camus placed at the front of his book:

> Dear soul, yearn not
> for eternal life,
> but fully embrace the possible.
>
> Pindar, Third Pythian Ode

This attitude stands in contrast to the attitude of flight, whether into illusion or death. Of course humans are prone to flee as well. Many myths and folk tales could be listed in which gods, goddesses, heroes and heroines are running away. But the Sisyphus myth is not about a person in flight; this is a person who stands his ground and gives everything he can.

Camus argues further that the universe no longer has a master. This argument seems a bit strange. For Camus says Sisyphus has abolished the gods by accepting his punishment and neither whining for mercy nor running away. But we know that Sisyphus is still being punished by these gods. Though there is no god, says Camus, this universe is "neither sterile nor worthless." [5] "Every grain of this boulder, every mineral chip of this mountain full of night, alone forms a whole world. The struggle towards the summits is enough in itself to fulfill a human heart. We must imagine Sisyphus happy." [6]

Camus' view of the myth opens up a fascinating facet of Sisyphus. He is a model of a person who has no hope of success or change in his situation, yet fulfills his assignment, regardless of the fact that it is considered to be a punishment. Thus Sisyphus is a model for all of those situations in which people who don't hope for change simply do whatever is closest at hand to be done. To be sure, they retain the hope that some day their fate will turn. Are we surprised by such heroism? Do we admire it? If we look more closely this heroism becomes problematical.

According to Camus it is not only dedication to the task, without the prospect of success, that motivates Sisyphus. It is also the fact that through his efforts he eliminates the power of the gods. He proves that compared to the gods, he is the stronger. Viewed from the perspective of depth psychology, we have here a person who accomplishes a task through the application of all his ego strength or will. Sadly, however, he can never allow himself to weaken or to be inspired by anything else. Sisyphus enjoys nothing but his exertion. He is a person who exhibits exceptional exertion in order to show that he can do anything that he wants by himself. He has no unconscious tendencies that run contrary to his conscious intentions. He always keeps things under control. And yet he fails repeatedly.

If we view Sisyphus as a model hero for the human being according to Existentialism (a suggestion by Bollnow[7]), the mythological image reveals both the strength and weakness of this philosophy. The strength resides in standing up for oneself, in never giving up, and in taking charge of one's own fate instead of constantly allowing oneself to be represented by another person or god. The responsibility for oneself, even without the prospect of success is plain to see. No matter what one's fate may be, one can bring about change by doing whatever is possible.

This perspective is vital, especially for psychotherapists. We often find ourselves with patients who begin to understand how much their present behavior has to do with their experiences in childhood. They constantly make father, mother or fate "responsible" for their present-day difficulties, a strategy that only serves to push the principle of responsibility for oneself further into the background. In such cases the responsibility theme of Existentialism can act as a corrective: We must do whatever lies within our power to change our lives.

The weakness of Existentialism is revealed by what is absent in this model. The myth of Sisyphus completely lacks eros, the sphere of love and relationship to people. Also missing in the story is the ability to let go in life, the ability to devote oneself to and trust anything other than one's own strength and will.

In view of all that is missing in Camus' Myth of Sisyphus we must also leave aside any consideration of hope or of metaphysics. It is not pure coincidence that at approximately the same time as Camus published Sisyphus, Gabriel Marcel released *The Philosophy of Hope.*[8] In contrast to Camus' exclusive emphasis on the here and now and the capability of the human will, Marcel affirms trusting, hoping and the mystery of love. Thus hope becomes the polar opposite of presumption and defiance. Camus and Marcel present us with two different aspects of human nature. Each of these attitudes can be essential in a particular situation. Both attitudes taken together and the tension which exists between them, seem to me to define the human condition.

If in his explanation Camus would only say that a man who is condemned by the gods to an absurd fate embraces this fate and works with it and thereby defies the gods, I would have little objection to his theory, though it would still seem awfully difficult to accomplish the task without any hope whatsoever. There are periods in every person's life during which one has to adopt this attitude in order to survive. It is this very attitude, even in coping with everyday things, that gives one the strength to live with what fate has dished out. Indeed, one can experience one's own strength for the first time by rising to the occasion and coping with a difficult task.

But when Camus also adds that one should picture

Sisyphus

Sisyphus as a happy man, I wonder why on earth he
introduces this theme here. If Camus were to say that he
views his hero as living life with the greatest intensity
(*vivre le plus*), as living it with daring, I would gladly go
along with his argument. But happy? Wouldn't "digni-
fied" be the more accurate word?

I do not wish here to enter into either an appreciation
or a criticism of Existentialism as represented by Camus.
This text is too slim a basis for that. Neither do I wish to
consider whether or not Sisyphus is or was a happy man. I
am only concerned with formulating the issue of hope or
hopelessness.

That seems to me to be a central question, in the way
that I consider hope and hopelessness to be central emo-
tions in human life. Naturally hope implies a view toward
the future, toward change, and therefore toward creative
transformation. Hope gives us wings. Hope consoles us.
But sometimes it also distracts us and hinders us in actually achieving what is possible. We may hope for future
transformation instead of tackling what needs to be
changed in the present. This sometimes gives hope a bad
reputation.

But hoping is not just timidly waiting for an "opportunity" to present itself or building castles in the air. Hoping
is ultimately trusting that there is a solid foundation in
our lives, and that our own intentions can be brought into
a coherent relationship with the entirety of life. In hope
there is ultimately a form of security. Hope transcends the
here and now and the conscious will. Hope generally
gives us the strength to take on a task in the confidence
that sooner or later something will change or that at least
there is some sense in persevering.

Is Sisyphus supposed to have summoned up this immense energy again and again, in spite of all his failure
and without any hope? If we consider Camus' argument
more carefully it appears that even Sisyphus does not end

up entirely without hope. To be sure, Sisyphus knows that he will never arrive at a conclusion, and since he is already in the Hereafter the repetition must be considered "eternal." So he has no illusions. But his "happiness" Sisyphus draws from the fact that he holds his own in the "struggle towards the summits." Therefore he must continue to hope that he will hold his own in the struggle toward the summits again and again. It follows that his actions during this struggle become essential for him, for they give Sisyphus the experience of his own strength along the road that has no goal. So even for Camus Sisyphus doesn't make it without hope. But he hopes only for the continuity of his own strength, not for something to transcend him as the man of will and ultimately help him along.

In the final analysis, we will never know whether Sisyphus had hope or not. The myth today can only be understood as it has been enriched with reflections from our own lives. Nevertheless, I cannot see Sisyphus simply as a person who endures an eternal repetition entirely without hope. That seems to me a grandiose idea demanding too much of a person. Sisyphus is an overtaxed hero.

I can imagine that even though Sisyphus knows that the gods have told him he will never reach the goal, he still secretly hopes to reach it after all. He is challenged by this pronouncement of the gods, the way a clear rejection of our capabilities can sometimes stimulate us to achieve something immediately in defiance, as a sort of heroic and hopeful gesture against apparent defeat. Defiance is after all an important source of strength for people. Quite often we develop out of defiance against a prediction that was not very flattering to us. In defiance we often come to experience our potential strengths, because we finally stand up for ourselves. Sisyphus is a defiant hero. When the myth is considered in this way, Sisyphus is still concerned with coming to grips with fate and the gods, but it is a much more open grappling than Camus postulated.

Sisyphus does not despise the gods; he sees them as a measure of himself. He has to prove his will to persevere and his dignity by dealing repeatedly with disillusionment.

The myth does not therefore center on the person who lives on in hopelessness, accepts his absolute limitation and, despising death, creates as much of life as is possible for him. The myth stresses instead the person who *hopes*, who exerts himself, is disappointed again and again and yet refuses to run away. Still hoping, he starts over again and thus ultimately wrests a bit more of life away from death.

Disappointment involves having to abandon a conception that we have had. We have expected something that did not occur. We have not just *hoped for* something, but have *expected* it. Expectation is much narrower than hope. It is to a greater extent centered on an event around which we define ourselves. If what is expected does not occur, then we lose our center. We call the feeling that accompanies this loss disappointment. Often it is the disappointment which first makes clear to us the nature of the expectation and the fact that this expectation can perhaps never be fulfilled. Here the important question arises as to how to deal with this disappointment.

Sisyphus is a model for the person who engages himself again in spite of disappointment. He takes up the stone again and starts over as if the loss had never happened. In Sisyphus' situation a person who is less resilient would come to a halt on the top of the mountain and complain, even if he had been forewarned that he would be disappointed. It would be hard for him to risk the new beginning. After all, he could be disappointed all over again. But Sisyphus can defiantly work through the disappointment and the accompanying emotional hurt. He does not let disappointment hinder him from coping with life. To this extent he wrests a bit of life away from death. Sisyphus is not just a hero who is not easily hurt; he is a hero of great strength, a hero with great energy.

The myth does not speak of our hero's disappointment. We hear nothing about how he makes his way down into the fields, which might have given us a clue as to how he experiences and deals with defeat. The myth says only that he begins anew. Insofar as we are willing to identify with Sisyphus, he gives us, too, the courage to start over, even when it is the same old burden that has to be shouldered.

If we contemplate this myth not in terms of hope and hopelessness, but in terms of expectation and the disappointment which comes with it, then the heroic deed of Sisyphus remains undiminished, but he is no longer an absurd hero. To repeatedly take risks in life, though we know that a disappointment is always possible, means to adopt a larger frame of reference and accept that we must continue to say good-bye to certain conceptions and expectations without giving up. All of us know how much strength and how much courage that can take.

Recurrent Disappointments and Renewed Hope

Let us consider relationships in this context. After all, in relationships we have more than the usual number of expectations, and more than the usual number are dashed. When we are disappointed we do not want to be cast indefinitely in the victim's role, so we enter into the relationship again, in the certain knowledge that some sort of disappointment, perhaps even the same one, will occur again. This action represents a constructive realization of the Sisyphus theme.

There is a particularly penetrating depiction of this theme in Ingeborg Bachmann's story "Undine Goes."* Undine settles her accounts with men. In her tally sheet it

---

* Undine is a mermaid in German folk tales whose semi-human nature dooms her to unsatisfying encounters with men.

strikes us that for her all men bear the same name and the same desires, and with each the same experience starts over from the beginning.

> You people! You monsters!
> You monsters with the name Hans! – with this name that I can never forget.
> Every time I came through the clearing and the twigs opened up, when the brush knocked the water off my arms and the leaves licked the drops from my hair, I ran into someone whose name was Hans.
> Yes, I've learned this logic, that a person has to be named Hans, that you are all named Hans, each one like the other. But there is really only one of you. It is always just one who bears this name, one that I can't forget, even if I forget all of you, completely and utterly forget you, just as I once loved you completely. When your kisses and your seed have long since been washed off and flushed away by the many great waters, the rains, rivers and oceans, the name remains with me. It propagates itself under water, because I can't stop calling it, Hans, Hans ...[9]

> Being nowhere, staying nowhere. Diving, resting, moving without the expenditure of energy – and one day remembering, emerging at the surface again, entering a clearing, seeing him and saying 'Hans.' Starting from the beginning.
> 'Good evening.'
> 'Good evening.'
> 'How far is it to you?'
> 'Far, it is far.'
> 'And it is far to me.'
> Always repeating the same mistake, the one mistake by which one is known.[10]

In relationships one makes the same mistake over and over, the one "by which one is known." This wonderful expression suggests that these mistakes mark us, but they also make us special. They are our distinguishing feature, making us unique.

And naturally Undine too makes the mistake for which she is known. After she has settled accounts with the monsters, she says:

> But I can't go like this. Therefore let me speak well of you again, so that we don't part like this. So that there is no real parting.[11]

Here the problematic aspect of Undine's behavior is revealed. There are situations in which we clearly slip into a compulsion to repeat. We strive with increasing energy to attain the same thing, generally from our partner. We simply cannot refrain from hoisting what is really the same boulder with precisely the same effort and the same strategy.

An Example: Senseless Expectation

A man had married a very deeply depressed woman. He made it his life task to relieve her depression. At the same time he could transfer his own depressive elements to her and do battle with them in her. He spoiled her, did everything for her, massaged her, inspired her. Sometimes he suffered greatly, because his own needs were no longer taken into account. Every once in a while his wife told him she simply couldn't go on any more, and every time that happened, he was gravely disappointed. He didn't let his disappointment show, however, and continued to set up new programs, torturing himself even further and believing that this time he was bound to succeed. But of course he didn't succeed. In his care she had no opportunity to test and strengthen herself, to develop the ability to shoulder her own stone.

I have included this example here to illustrate that Sisyphean behavior is really not appropriate for all occasions. It must be applied in the right life situation. The courage to begin anew, which is also courage to bear our losses, can be simply a compulsion to repeat. It can be a blind urge to prove our own will superior, a mere expression of the fact that we are both unable and unwilling to give up.

THE STONE AS A SYMBOL

The stone symbolizes more than simply that which resists, opposes or repulses us. It is more, too, than a mere burden. The solid and almost changeless character of the stone renders it a symbol of firmness and immutability and thus also of reliability. Resistance is an important part of this reliability. Only something which can offer resistance is firm enough to be relied upon in time of need.

Because of their indestructibility, firmness and reliability stones have come to symbolize both gods and concentrated divine power. Meteorites, the stones from space which literally "fall from heaven," have always been viewed as an expression of the nearness of heaven to earth and connected with fertility. Furthermore, in ancient Greece before the gods were represented in human form, an unsculpted stone was considered a symbol for Hermes or Apollo.[12]

At first it looks as if the myth incorporates only the resistance, bulk and weight of this stone – this stone that demands the supreme exertion of the person who seeks to move it. I believe, however, that we should not neglect the more extended symbolism of the stone as a god-image. We should consider more than just the burden and the exertion aspects of the Sisyphus experience. We could include in our interpretation of the myth the bearing of the *god* which is associated with the stone, and thereby embrace the particular life task incorporated in each god.

If the rock were Hermes, then we would explore the

themes of creativity and transformation. For Hermes guards gates and doors, protects travelers and those who cross borders, and leads the way into the underworld. He is equipped with inventiveness and a roguish wit, and for this reason too he is the god who oversees transitions and transformations. At first glance a god whose realm is that of change seems to be a stark contrast to Sisyphus. We will deal more with Hermes later.

If we were dealing with Apollo there would be several possible interpretations. Apollo changed his meaning often. Originally a guardian of gates like Hermes, he became increasingly a god of healing and atonement. Later his son Asclepius took over his healing aspect. Closely connected to healing was the gift of prophecy. Apollo spoke to people through the mouth of his inspired prophetess. Since the sixth century before Christ he has also been worshipped as Helios, the god of the sun. He is not then just a god of light, for he guarantees order and balance, too.[13]

Thus healing and atonement could be burdens which Sisyphus must bear. Connected to these could also be prophecy, balance and the theme of the sun that continues to rise perpetually.

The myth of Sisyphus did not originate in early antiquity. Therefore the amplification, the extended symbolism of the stone which I am bringing to it, is only valid if we accept that earlier forms of expression can be superseded by later myths. What I wish to emphasize here is that the rock is more than just a burden. It is also an assigned task, associated in Greek times with the carrying of a god. Thus Sisyphus work is an exertion which ultimately facilitates the breakthrough of something divine in a human being.

In spite of my amplification the fact remains that in the eyes of his chroniclers Sisyphus has no success. He strains and struggles without end and without any prospect of liberation. If one were to find any "success," it would have to lie precisely in that unceasing striving.

Now the matter no longer seems so entirely senseless. Sisyphus does what is humanly possible with the life task which has been assigned to him. He can do no more. He cannot master the task in the truest sense of the word. He can only stick with it. But now this perseverance is of a different sort. It has to do with hope, hope for meaning. For Sisyphus does not simply bear a burden, he shoulders a task which brings him into connection with the divine. Here, as in previous interpretations, the meaning does not lie in the completion of the task, but in the process. It is the ground that is repeatedly covered with this "stone" as well as the experiences that are gathered along the way that are important. In the case of Sisyphus they are experiences of strength and power.

Thus it is possible to interpret the stone either as a burden or as a person's assigned task. Other meanings are possible, too. For me the interpretation points toward this question: If we view the act of pushing the stone as a common human situation, do we understand the stone simply as an unmovable burden that does nothing but weigh us down, disturbing and demanding all our strength without meaning? Or do we seek to find life tasks in the stones that we shoulder, though they are sometimes unpleasant? Do we seek to find the meaning in the situation, to the extent sometimes that we invent one?

These two possible interpretations have something in common. In the largest problems that we have lies our greatest potential for development. The difficulties we encounter are a constant challenge and thereby provoke our development.

Now to look at an aspect that has been repeatedly touched upon in the discussion of this myth: It is not as important to attain the goal as it is to be on the road to it. Of course the road leads to that desired goal. What is important, however, is not reaching the goal but the engagement in the process and the courage to be able to start over from the beginning again and again.

THE PRECONDITION FOR THE PUNISHMENT

The First Part of the Myth of Sisyphus

So far we have focused our attention on the punishment of Sisyphus. This aspect of punishment is much more accessible to us than the little known earlier part of the story. Now we must ask how it came about that Sisyphus was being punished. The prehistory will shed light on some of our previous lines of interpretation.

Roscher writes that the word "Sisyphos" means simply "the clever one." [14] According to the Iliad (Book 6, line 152), Sisyphus, who lived in Corinth in the corner of horsepasturing Argos, was considered to be one of the cleverest and most devious of men.

The collection of all the things he is supposed to have done is confusing. I quote here from the text of the *Dictionary of Antique Myths and Figures.*

Sisyphus was the son of Aeolus and Enarete. He founded the city of Corinth, which he originally named Ephyra. His cleverness and skill were proverbial. For this reason he was sometimes connected with the master thief Autolycus (by those with no concern for the chronological order of legends). Later story-tellers claimed that Autolycus had stolen his herds, but Sisyphus won them back. Sisyphus had cut notches in the hooves and thus could disprove the denials of Autolycus. Sisyphus then avenged himself against the thief by seducing his daughter Anticleia. That is the source of the occasional rumor that Sisyphus, and not Anticleia's husband

Laertes, was the father of Odysseus, to whom she subsequently gave birth.

When Sisyphus founded Ephyra, he established the Isthmus games in honor of Melicertes, whose body he had found and buried there. He also fortified the neighboring heights of Acrocorinth as a citadel and a watchtower. One day by chance he caught sight of Zeus just as he was carrying off the river nymph Aegina, the daughter of the river god Asopus and Metope. Zeus bore her to the island of Oinone, where he deflowered her. Asopus took up the chase and asked Sisyphus for information. The latter promised to tell what he knew if he would receive a fresh water spring in Acrocorinth in return, which Asopus promptly provided (the Peirene spring). Zeus was angry about Sisyphus' revelation and wanted to punish him. He sent Thanatos (Death) to bring Sisyphus to the house of Hades (god of the underworld). Somehow the clever Sisyphus outwitted Thanatos, tied him up and threw him in a prison, after which mortals ceased to die. Threatened by this unnatural condition, the gods sent out Ares (the god of war) to set Thanatos free.

Then Thanatos sought out Sisyphus for a second time. Sisyphus had prepared his wife, the Pleiad Merope, with precise instructions for this contingency: She left his body unburied and offered none of the usual sacrifices to the dead man. In this way Sisyphus outwitted Hades. The god of the underworld was so enraged over Merope's negligence that either he or his consort Persephone allowed Sisyphus to return to the upper world in order to punish Merope and arrange for the burial of the corpse. Once back in Corinth Sisyphus did nothing of the kind, but rejoiced in his life and lived to a very old age, laughing at the gods of the underworld. It was probably because of this godlessness, as well as his betrayal of Zeus – so it was assumed – that his shade was tortured in Tartarus after his death. He was forced to roll a large boulder constantly up a hill. Each time he almost reached the top it rolled back down again.

After a long life Sisyphus was buried on the Isthmus of Corinth. He left behind four sons, Glaucus (father of Bellerophon), Ornytion (father of Phocos 2), Thersandrus and Almus.[15]

The deeds of Sisyphus described here are mentioned in all of the relevant reference works, though sometimes they are evaluated differently. At the center of these deeds stands the outwitting of death.

If one looks at all of his acts, one is convinced that Sisyphus must have been an extraordinarily cunning, skillful, and clever man, but also a man of courage. He chose to fight with the gods, and he was a force to be reckoned with. From this point of view one can interpret the punishment in the underworld to mean that the gods are stronger than Sisyphus after all. Do we have here a simple power struggle between a human and the gods? Is it symbolic of the way in which, in confrontation with the gods, a human carves out a rich life for himself and is ultimately punished for it?

Or are the mythographers simply trying to construct a punishment and its justification as a warning to people? Could the mythmakers have been concerned that individuals who take after Sisyphus would become arrogant enough to challenge the gods to the extent where they become gods themselves, a condition which is not proper for humans?

In this way one could explain why a colorful succession of tricks and misdeeds were attributed to Sisyphus. He has obviously been made into an example in which the question of the proper proportions for humankind is presented for all eyes to see.

SISYPHUS, THE TRICKSTER

Sisyphus is a master thief. He succeeds in recovering his stolen goods and in catching and convicting *the* master thief who owes his skills directly to Hermes. Sisyphus therefore shows himself to be more cunning than the supposed master thief, Autolycus. Hermes had granted Autolycus the gift of being able to turn stolen horned cattle into hornless, black cattle into white and vice versa.[16] Thus Hermes plays a role in explaining the essence of Sisyphus. We therefore turn our attention to him first.

Piles of stones and gravestones were sacred to Hermes. From them came later the Herms, the stone pillars which protected Greek houses and were viewed as the residence of the god. Hermes was a god who was always on the road. He was not only the god of the traveler and wanderer. As messenger of the gods he also connected heaven with earth. As conductor of the dead, he connected earth with the underworld. Cleverness is an essential aspect of his character. Hermes, too, is labeled a master thief, for he was scarcely born when he stole a herd of cattle from his brother Apollo. Making lucky discoveries and taking them for oneself are also conditions associated with Hermes. Therefore he is a god of inventions and inventors. He is also responsible for invention in the intellectual sphere and for interpretation and explanation (Hermeneutics). Among other things Hermes is said to have invented the game of dice and from that the art of prophecy.[17] Thus he is the patron-saint of inventors, intellectuals, public speakers, thieves and merchants. But he is also the one who sends us dreams and probably the one who stimulates us to dream.

Hermes is one of the "divine children" of mythology. As such he is an expression of the perennial possibility of new beginnings throughout life. He represents an untamable life force. In addition to this he bears traits of a fertility god: The stones in the fields could be the expression of a pre-Greek fertility cult, which connects him to the Great Mother. He is as much at home in the real world as in the sky and the underworld. Thus he is a god who brings about connections and transitions and thereby promises creative transformation. He is forever roving, always in motion. He is and remains a young god, never aging because he is always on the move. He is connected with the emotion of hope, with the certainty that somehow everything finds a solution. Hermes is a god of the moment and of connections, and the consequences of his deeds seem not to concern him.

He is also a master thief. Therefore he can show others how to become master thieves. Plato writes in the *Phaedrus* that each person belongs to the retinue of a particular god and honors that god by imitating him or her in life.[18]

From this point of view Sisyphus is, without a doubt, a person who lives "in the retinue" of Hermes. He leads a life that is very clearly imprinted with the capabilities and peculiarities of this god. The Greek way of thinking has been lost to us for a very long time. We consider ourselves to have either good or bad qualities of character. When someone demonstrates an unusual and striking characteristic we are quick to label it abnormal, perhaps even pathological. We might be able to cope better with our distinguishing peculiarities if we could view them as the effect of a god in our lives or as the expression of something essential to the life of the individual.

Let us now observe in Sisyphus the characteristics that have been determined by Hermes.

The Master Thief

We are familiar with the master thief from folk tales. He is a figure who has always been of interest. These folk tales always begin with parents who have a son who would rather play silly tricks than work. This son is chased away or disappears of his own accord. Years later he returns as a distinguished gentleman; he has become a success. The man reveals himself. In each story he goes then to the king or count, his godfather, and at the other man's command steals something like the count's best horse, perhaps by appearing disguised as a woman and getting the servants drunk. Then, again at the invitation of the count, he steals the sheet and wedding ring of the countess. To accomplish this he first cuts down a dead man from the gallows and then puts up a ladder to the bedroom of the count, who of course sees it. The master thief pushes the corpse up the ladder, and the count shoots the man who is already dead. He has him buried quickly. Meanwhile the master thief approaches the countess, disguised as the count, and requests the wedding ring and sheet as donations for the grave of the godson. As final proof of his art he is to lock the preacher and the sexton of the neighboring community into a chicken coop without using force. The master thief collects crabs for a whole day. Then he sticks little burning lights between the crabs' pincers and lets them loose to run around the cemetery at night. At the same time he preaches that the time of prophecy has been fulfilled; people need only look to the churchyard. Whoever wished to enter heaven should crawl quickly into the sack he carries, because there is not much room in it. Of course the preacher and the sexton are the first to crowd their way into the sack.

The count gives him money and asks him to go away to another country, because he is too dangerous to have around.[19]

This type of folk tale with minor variations is very widely known. If one succeeds in looking at this tale without moralizing, it is clear that the master thief is not primarily interested in making himself rich, but rather in the amusement of the challenge to outfox another person. The craftiest is the one who wins the contest. These master thieves are extraordinarily imaginative fairy-tale heroes. On the one hand they have very creative inspirations. On the other hand they have perfect mastery of the art of deception: They can feel their way into the minds of other people and predict what they will do. It is a contest, a competition of creative inspiration. That these master thieves also get rich is merely a lucky coincidence. Nevertheless none of them have a place where they can stay, like Hermes, whom they somehow take after. They are always sent on their way again, gathering experiences as they go.

By catching Autolycus in the act of robbery, Sisyphus goes beyond proving that he is superior to the master thief. He even manages to get the thief to quarrel with the witnesses while he seduces his daughter.[20] This liaison is supposed to have resulted in Odysseus, whose wanderings can thus be understood as fated from the outset. Ultimately, it remains unclear who seduced whom in this affair.

Thus Sisyphus could be a model for the person with creative inspiration who uses it to take advantage of other people. The quick creative deed that brings about a change is more important to him than the consequences. He is provoked into tricking Autolycus, because he cannot stand by and have his herds stolen. Once provoked, Sisyphus successfully applies all of his resources to defend what belongs to him.

The Bartered Spring

Sisyphus is watching when Zeus carries off the daughter of the river god. Aesopus looks for her, and Sisyphus is willing to give him the information in return for a spring on the previously barren hill next to Corinth which is called Acrocorinth. Sisyphus receives this spring, which also bears other legends about its origin. Thus he proves himself to be a very skillful bargainer: information in exchange for water. A spring on waterless Acrocorinth must have been very important, for water means life and fertility, not just for Sisyphus but for the entire city. Sisyphus takes advantage of the distress of a god to attain something that provides him and his fellow humans with an increase in life, symbolically a greater vitality. He was simply in the right place at the right time, and he was alert to possibilities.

Sisyphus is willing to betray the Olympian Zeus to the river god, the god of water and eternal flowing, in order to obtain the latter's favor. This favor manifests itself in the spring that wells up out of the ground. The spring stands for the overflowing riches of Mother Earth, symbolizing fertility and the abundance of life. By doing this, however, Sisyphus makes an enemy of Zeus.

Sisyphus doesn't really care that he is courting the disfavor of Zeus, though as the highest god Zeus is lord over all other gods and men, demands obedience and crushes all resistance. Sisyphus is prepared to take on Zeus, if only because the god's demands concern him less than what is useful and pleasing to him and the city which he founded. He is interested not in obedience, but in life. He wants to be a follower not of Zeus, but of the river god, a god who personifies eternal transformation and flux, and thus constant change.

If we see him as a model for humans, Sisyphus is attracted to eternal change, as is clearly represented in flowing water. He is gripped by creative transformation. If Sisyphus represents the creative person, then this image expresses the basic conflict of every creative person. No one can be creative and at the same time fully respect the old order. Everything creative stands in opposition to an established order and struggles with it. No wonder Zeus feels himself challenged.

The drastic nature of the punishment shows just how threatened Zeus feels by Sisyphus. He is to die immediately.

Death is Outwitted

The motif of outwitting death is also a familiar one in folk tales. In some variants death is replaced by the devil. As examples I would like to introduce two types of folk tales. The first type can be represented by the French tale "How Death Was Fooled."

A saint gave to a woman one wish for her worthy deeds. She expressed the wish that she could catch and hold fast everyone who climbed up into her plum tree to take plums. The saint fulfilled this strange wish. Ten years later Death came by her house and wanted to take her with him. She declared herself ready to go along, but requested that before she went she first be allowed to eat some plums. Death climbed up into the tree to bring down some plums for her. And the woman said, "I wish that Death may not get down from the tree without my permission."

Death flew into a passion, pleaded, threatened and screamed. He could not get down again. No one else on earth would die. All the feeble, wounded and sick people suffered terribly, because they could not die. People came from all over to plead with the woman to let Death go. Finally she agreed on condition that she would have to call Death three times before he could come to her again.[21]

This type of folk tale comes closest to the story that is told of Sisyphus. Once again it is a story in which cunning plays a great role, cunning and the desire to have control over death, to abolish mortality.

This example also makes clear what happens when Death is held captive. Nothing can change, and nothing can be brought to an end. That, too, causes suffering. Secret pleasure nevertheless can be derived from the fact that though this destroyer cannot be destroyed, he can be captured. That suggests immense triumph of human power over the laws of life, or over the gods, if we stick to the language of myth. The woman in the French folk tale gains control over Death thanks to a wish she was granted for her virtuous conduct. Sisyphus achieves the same goal with his cleverness, and probably his bodily strength. He does not accept the punishment that Zeus has thought up for him. He puts Death out of commission. But in so doing he also suspends the principle of transience, the second principle of the creative belonging inseparably to the first. Ares, the violent fighter among the gods who acts in the service of destructive change, has to come to the aid of Death.

If we try to view Sisyphus as a model for a person, then it is of a man who is so convinced of his own power, his intelligence and his ability to be creative that he believes himself immortal. Death, change, setbacks and having to let go, these things hold no reality for him. When he is threatened by the principle of "death" we see this attitude most clearly in his behavior – he chains up death and locks it away in a storage room. By this action our friend sets himself up as equal to Zeus, on the same level as the gods. But in so doing he suspends the principle that makes the creative possible. Ares, the god who incorporates the principles of battle and aggression, reverses the results of this skulduggery. The gods are thus superior to Sisyphus after all.

Ares' intervention shows that death is effective even for Sisyphus. One can understand death as the announcement of old age. Or one can see in it the coming of things to an end, the other face of the creative. Let us not forget the fact that Sisyphus followed the god Hermes, an eternally youthful god, and follows him still. For that reason he must battle against death, but he cannot deny totally the principle of destruction. That is probably why he seeks to outwit death yet a second time. This is what makes it possible for him to grow old.

Death is Outwitted Once Again

Here once again Sisyphus proves himself to be far-sighted, knowing what will happen even before he acts. He knows the reactions of the gods of the underworld. He has his wife fail to bury his corpse and bring offerings to the dead. This infuriates the gods. For by doing this Sisyphus directs his wife to reject the gods of the underworld by withholding her sacrifices. At the command of Sisyphus she too refuses to take death into account. She simply rejects it. The gods of the underworld send Sisyphus back to the world in order to reinstate the customs. Naturally he does not return to the underworld. He becomes a very old man and continues to laugh at the gods. Twice Sisyphus has triumphed over death and proven himself more clever than the gods. His laughter at the gods shows that setting himself against the gods and proving himself superior has a central meaning in this myth.

The ruse of refusing the sacrificial offerings can only succeed with the help of our hero's wife. This is the only time that his wife is ever mentioned. Other than that she plays no part in the story. The "assignment" which Sisyphus is given, yet which he also chooses for himself is competition with the gods, above all with the god of death. By winning, Sisyphus can live in the world and grow old. He can laugh at these gods. They choose not to renew the battle. It should have been easy for them to catch Sisyphus again, but perhaps they were too unnerved to try. Or perhaps they were wise, in the knowledge that the hour of death strikes sooner or later for every mortal, and their hour would come.

This ruse of Sisyphus appears in a comparable form in the Icelandic folk tale, "The King's Son and Death":

Once an unknown master promised to teach a king's son such wise things as no other person could learn. The king's son sat in silence with the wise man in the forest and studied with this silent master. After three years the wise man revealed to the youth that he was Death himself. The position he took at the bed of a sick person determined the duration of the sickness, and whether the patient would recover or die. Death then gave his student some knowledge of medication. The king's son became a famous doctor and in his time became king. One day when he was a hundred years old he saw his old master sitting by his head, and he knew this was a sign that he was to die. The king asked the master to postpone his death until he could pray the paternoster. He said only the first four parts of the prayer, however, and then explained that he would finish it only when he was tired of living. Death was outwitted and had to leave him. A hundred years later, life began to be a burden to the king, so he completed the paternoster and died.[23]

The central theme of both types of folk tales is the outwitting of death. Their dynamic is that of proving oneself superior to death, though this can only ever be achieved temporarily. Ultimately death cannot be overcome. The goal is to evade death until one is truly satiated with life.

The folk tale "How Death Was Fooled" is concerned above all with cunning, in this case the ability of a person to keep death waiting. It is the ability to make available as much time and intensity as possible for living which is stressed. Understood in one way, this is the determination to live life as intensively as possible at all times, refusing to give up, even in the face of inevitable death. One can view this death both as the process of dying, and as the principle of withering away. Thus, outwitting death could be viewed as the refusal to give up the zest for life too early while retaining the awareness that everything must pass away ultimately. In the Sisyphus myth, this attitude would be a refusal to quit pushing the boulder too soon. Understood another way, outwitting death could also be seen as a refusal to accept the inevitability of death and the passing of time, which are part of the necessity of letting go, starting over, and thus the principle of repetition.

In the folk tale "The King's Son and Death," as well as in the Grimm's fairy tale of Godfather Death [24] it is a doctor who outwits death. He has studied with Death, who presented himself as a mysterious wise man. Thus Death, himself, teaches us how to cope with him. The folk tale, "The King's Son and Death," showed that every sickness can be understood as the presence of death, though it does not necessarily lead to death. In these tales Death himself seems to challenge us to offer resistance. He even shows us the means to employ.

In all folk tales of this type, however, Death sets up clear limits to the ability of an individual to heal the sick. Thus in both tales a dual attitude with regard to death is expressed: on the one hand we find the quest to obtain for oneself as much of life as possible; on the other hand is the recognition that in certain situations there is no alternative to death and, figuratively, to the necessity of letting go. Naturally these doctors try each time to outwit Death. In the Grimm's fairy tale of Godfather Death it happens when the doctor quickly turns the bed of the sick person around. For that the doctor dies himself. When these doctors overreach the limits in the application of the gift which they have received from Godfather Death and put themselves in the position of lord over life and death, Death ultimately determines the human lot and crushes the immoderate expectation. But Death himself seems to challenge humanity to the ruse, and he accepts it each time he is outwitted. Actually outwitting Death is taking death very seriously. Death stimulates our greatest efforts to keep life exciting. In the folk tales, however, one can always outwit Death only for a certain period of time. And thus it is for Sisyphus, too. Even though he is allowed to live to a ripe old age, ultimately he must die.

RETURN TO THE STONE

The myth tells us quite clearly: Because Sisyphus has outwitted death twice his shade must roll the boulder in the underworld. He is not able to stop rolling the stone, and yet he is forced to let it go again and again. This life theme of having to sustain the effort while at the same time having to let go repeatedly, this theme of eternal repetition, is repeated here incessantly.

Sisyphus sought to outwit death, to prevent something from coming to an end, to avoid having to let go. And now in the realm of the shades his torture will never come to an end and he will never escape. He cannot give up rolling the stone, and yet he must continue to let it go. The central theme of his earthly life repeats itself here in the world of the shades, the unwillingness to accept the passing away of all things and yet acceptance of this inevitability. Even now Sisyphus engages his will to fight in the face of this transience. He still refuses to let go voluntarily. He lets go only when the excessive weight of the stone overwhelms him. He is unable to let go, and therefore he repeatedly has something taken away from him. His wish remains to outwit death. But what in the world of the living had been such a playful task accomplished with levity and without great effort has now become an extreme hardship.

Sisyphus reminds us of the situation in which many doctors find themselves. To a great extent we delegate to doctors the role of fighting death. Not only are they to postpone the "final death" as long as possible, they should preserve us in eternal youth if they can. These demands which we make of them, and which they make great efforts to fulfill, must be a great burden to some.

Previously in the comparison with the folk tales which I introduced to illustrate the myth, it became clear that the ultimate question was this: When is it sensible to preserve for oneself this "additional life" and refuse to let go, and when is it time to agree to a loss or a departure? Sisyphus never gave his assent, and it is his punishment that he will now never be able to give it. If we consider our hero's life history as far as it is told to us, we must conclude that we are dealing with a person who is oriented towards winning and unwilling to lose. He is so clever and full of tricks that he does not have to lose very much. Unlike Hermes, however, with whom he shares so many characteristics, Sisyphus is lacking the motif of the companion of the dead. He does not bring any dead souls into the under-world. Instead he shackles and outwits Death. He is a death-defying fighter who never gives up the struggle for a little more of life. As such, Sisyphus is an incredibly determined hero. But he is also a prisoner of his decision not to give up the fight against death.

The myth does not tell us when it makes sense to win more life away from death, to wrest it away with cunning and thus make it precious. It does not tell us how long it is sensible to struggle against the passing of time and against resignation. It also fails to indicate when it is more sensi-ble to consent to defeat. However, the myth is an example of what happens to us when we do not consent to a defeat. To be sure, we will not succeed as consistently as Sisyphus did in the first part of his story. If we never consent to a defeat, then, like Sisyphus, we must always wrestle the boulder up the mountain. And our boulder too will be-come too heavy and roll back down into the valley again resisting our every effort.

An Example:
The Refusal to Consent to a Loss

A forty-five-year-old man who has great potential and is gifted with the energy to realize much of that potential complains that he feels overburdened. He feels that he engages all of his talents and yet is unable to achieve anything that is authentic and valid for him. He can master only routine tasks. He toils, and everything is becoming too much for him. He cannot shake the sense that although he engages all his energy, he is not doing so correctly. This fellow would probably have to sacrifice something in order make progress, but he does not want to sacrifice anything. He believes that somehow, some day his full life potential and his capabilities will flow together into a whole, and that day will be the high point of his life.

This is a characteristic example of how the myth of Sisyphus can be translated and experienced in our daily lives. This man has many options in life, perhaps comparable to Sisyphus in his heyday. Every opportunity met, however, has its consequences. Each is the starting point of a chain of effects which tend to be connected to work. The day comes when the question of relinquishing something arises. Relinquishing means accepting that our abilities have limits, that human life is limited by death. But the man does not want to relinquish anything. He is gripped by the idea of being able to achieve something great at least once in his life, of actually bringing the stone to the peak. Because he is unable to leave anything behind, the burden of his work becomes heavier and heavier, and he feels himself to be further and further away from his yearned for "peak." Like Sisyphus he continues to renew his attempts to push the stone. But only a tired hope remains that he will ever achieve his peak experience in this way. He is increasingly filled with the certainty that something will have to be sacrificed.

Another Example of the Same Theme

A forty-nine-year-old woman, also highly gifted, didn't know quite rightly what she should concentrate on in her life. She was artistically talented in different areas, but she had a non-artistic profession. She could not make up her mind to do either one or the other. She lived a few years with art, returned to her profession and then turned to art again. Although relationships were very important to her, she didn't want to become settled down in them.

Now she, too, rolls a stone. She struggles with the question of the meaning of her life. Every time she thinks she has hit upon the meaning, she is unable to experience it. Her constant quest for meaning is the most consistent thing in her life, together with the refusal to decide in favor of something and therefore against something else, thus allowing a great part of her life to die.

The student whom I mentioned earlier cannot admit to his failure in his chosen field. Therefore he has to load himself down with an ever heavier boulder, which he can no longer push up the hill.

This is comparable to those situations in which we don't accept a failure as a manifestation of our limits, a guidepost that helps us to estimate our potential more realistically. Instead of learning from our failure to become more moderate with ourselves and allowing ourselves to be reminded of our limits, we are seized by the thought of wanting to make things better immediately. Thus we overreach or even handicap ourselves with our expectations.

If one tries to work out what is common in these examples, one sees that no matter how different they are and how differently they experience their stone, all of these people seem to be suffering without transformation. Just as Sisyphus continues to roll his stone, so they are rolling theirs. They cannot leave their situations behind and move toward change. In order to move, each would have to enter into a fundamental crisis which would force him to say good-bye to both illusions and real possibilities. All of these people are marked by a great stubbornness, a trait that shows they are followers of Sisyphus. Therefore we can calculate that as a result of the crisis new paths of life will be found, unless these people have so much energy to waste that even in the crisis they pick up and push their stones again with the same attitude. In doing this they could again be compared to Sisyphus. For he was in the underworld, but he came back to the upper world unchanged.

Change is only possible when we can let go and accept our losses.[25] Ultimately we must recognize that winning and losing are equally important aspects of life. In terms of the myth we need to recognize that we must be not only "master thieves" but "master losers."

Letting go demands more courage than holding on. After all, we never know how life will change when we let go. The myth only tells us what happens when we hold on beyond the time allotted to us. Letting go, however, can lead to the possibility of transformation.

An Example:
Letting Go Creates Freedom

A middle-aged couple had great problems in their relationship. When the children left home their difficulties became more acute as they became increasingly dependent upon each other. Both were of the opinion that separation or divorce were simply not feasible options for them. They tried hard to improve their relationship. They went out together, devised social programs and finally came into couple therapy.

In therapy it became clear that no matter how hard

they struggled to find common ground, to develop common interests and to offer at least friendly good will to one another, each continued to feel restricted and reacted allergically to every gesture by the other, whether verbal or physical in nature. When the woman complained that her husband always cleared his throat so unpleasantly, I pointed out that that was something which was unlikely to change. On the contrary, one would assume that this throat sound could only get more pronounced as life went on. This casual observation implied that she should take the partner simply for what he was at that moment and not as he might be if he were to fulfill all her demands. It had the effect that the woman suddenly wanted to talk about how a separation might be.

The rule that they had to stay together forever was thus set aside. Both renounced this security and sacrificed this expectation. Their sacrifice involved great anxiety. Both of them asked how those around them would react to such a move, how they would work things out alone, and so on.

As soon as the decision to contemplate separation was accepted by both of them each experienced greater freedom, and they began to approach each other in a completely different way. Suddenly they could share feelings with each other that they had never shared before.

One could view this development as a consequence of the fear of separation and of being alone that rose in them when they renounced the security of the formerly unassailable rule. However, the new development could also be interpreted to mean that the possibility of having to say good-bye brought out something in them which might enable them to live together. Naturally the two continued to have problems with each other, but they no longer tackled these problems from the basic supposition that the form of their relationship could not change. This change in their attitudes made it possible for them to approach problems in a much more relaxed manner.

The example above shows that in real life one can neither simply hold on nor simply let go. On the contrary, holding on and letting go are two sides of the same coin. Letting go without having previously held on is not really letting go. The focus of the Sisyphus myth is the attitude of a man who holds on because he cannot and will not let go. Viewed as a whole, however, the myth attributes to Sisyphus a counterforce against letting go too easily, against giving up. From the very beginning I have viewed pushing the stone in a dual way. On the one hand is the engagement that cannot be hindered by disillusionment, the stubbornness, the courageous constant return to the attack and the concentration, to name but a few of the key words. On the other is the aspect of fruitless struggle.

HOLDING ON AND LETTING GO

The courage to be stubborn and to engage oneself even when there is no chance of success, the attitude with which Camus was so impressed, is certainly experienced in this myth. For we hold on too tightly, and we often let go too soon. We resign ourselves to our lot, suffer from the futility of our efforts, and consider something hopeless when we have scarcely begun. This attitude can have numerous origins which I cannot examine here. It is an attitude that concedes more to death than to life, more to defeat than to victory and more to destruction than to creativity. It is a perspective that accentuates the fact that we all must die and gives everything in life the scent of mortality. Nothing is credited to the will, the power of decision and the human ego. Everything is attributed to evil fate. It is this attitude against which French Existentialist philosophy rebelled. In the face of war, situations in which people appear helplessly trapped, this philosophy challenged one to reject helplessness for as long as possible and to act with everything within one's own power, even if the task appeared hopeless.

This attitude is depicted most clearly in Camus' novel, *The Plague*. The plague breaks out in Oran. The inhabitants struggle relentlessly against the spreading epidemic. The plague changes everything about life in this city which quarantine has shut off from the outside world. For Rieux, the doctor, it goes without saying that he will do battle with the sickness as long as he can, though the same sequence of events keeps occurring and he cannot succeed in bringing about change:

> But lifting the coverlet and her nightshirt, he gazed in silence at the red spots on the girl's stomach and thighs and the swelling lymph nodes. The mother glanced between the legs of her daughter and shrieked, unable to control herself. Every evening mothers screamed like this, in distraction, as they caught sight of the fatal markings on limbs and bellies. Every evening Rieux's arms were clasped as useless words, promises and tears poured forth. Every evening the sounds of the ambulance touched off these attacks of despair as vain as every form of grief. And at the end of this long series of identical evenings Rieux could hope for nothing more than another series of similar scenes, repeated indefinitely. Yes, plague, like abstraction was monotonous. Only one factor changed, and that was Rieux himself. He sensed it that evening at the foot of the monument to the Republic. All he was conscious of was a bleak indifference steadily gaining on him as he gazed at the door of the hotel Rambert had just entered.[26]

Rieux battles against death even though he knows that he will lose. With the same attitude as Sisyphus he attempts to deny death its victims, and he tries to keep as many people as possible from being separated from their loved ones.

> 'After all,' the doctor repeated, then hesitated again, fixing his eyes on Tarrou, 'it is something that a man of your sort can understand most likely, but since the order of the world is shaped by death, mightn't it be better for God if we refused to believe in Him and struggle with all our might against death without raising our eyes towards the heaven where He sits in silence?'

Tarrou nodded, 'Yes. But your victories will never be lasting; that's all.'
Rieux's face darkened. 'Yes, I know. But that is no reason to give up the struggle.'
'No reason, I agree … Only, I now can picture what this plague must mean for you.'
'Yes,' said Rieux, 'a never-ending defeat.' [27]

In complete contrast to Rieux we find Rambert, a journalist who was in Oran by accident at the outbreak of the plague. He has a wife in Paris whom he loves and for whom he longs. He tries repeatedly to get out of the quarantined city. He chooses flight, and therefore his love. When it finally appears that there is an opportunity to flee, the people who were to help Rambert have become sick with the plague. Enraged, he realizes that he will have to start all over from the beginning, and suddenly he cries:

'No, you haven't understood that it [the plague] consists of just that, of starting over.' [28]

After Rambert has made this statement he decides to help Rieux in his volunteer medical service until he is able to leave the city. He, who had placed romantic love first, now chooses neighborly love. His beloved wife enters the city when the plague is defeated. What is impressive in the novel is that the battle against the plague continues even though it seems utterly hopeless. The more hopeless the situation appears, the more intensely the people struggle, and the more courageous they become in the hope of bringing the pestilence to a standstill.

But what does the plague symbolize? In the novel Camus puts these words into the mouth of an asthmatic who has escaped the plague: "But what does it mean anyway, this plague? It is life, nothing but that."

Very often the tendency to let go too soon is connected with a goal that has been set too high and is to be reached too quickly. It is true that Sisyphus is the model of an immoderate person, but such an "Anti-Sisyphus" is equally immoderate. The "antisisyphean" expectation is so immoderate that it is impossible to fulfill, and hence the energy that would be required to fulfill it cannot be released. Those with antisisyphean fantasies are often people who are extreme in their orientation toward their goals, but are filled with aversion by all the detours and repetitious efforts needed to reach them. When confronted with these unsatisfying situations they easily lose heart and give up everything for lost, including themselves.

Letting go, giving oneself up and holding some authority, "society," fate or a god responsible for everything that happens is an attitude against which we must constantly struggle.

In opposition to this attitude Sisyphus can serve as a model for the person who emphatically places his own force and will in the foreground and insists on the autonomy of his ego.[29] He takes everything upon himself, just to prove his independence. The myth suggests that such striving is not appropriate for a man. Nevertheless our hero embodies the opposite of the tendency to let go of everything, to yield up every life-giving impulse in the name of the relentless passing of time. On the contrary, he insists on being creative in the design of his life, even though we don't know the extent to which this is possible at any given time.

The existential themes that are addressed in the myth of Sisyphus are the polarities of autonomy and dependence, of expansion and moderation, and of insistence on one's own will and acceptance of limits. Ultimately the myth is about the necessity of creating a life in the face of death, whose presence has always been felt in the form of life changes. It is about the necessity to live as intensely as possible in the face of death while accepting inevitable changes.

In this context, however, the myth sheds light on only one part of life, and that is daily activity. After all, Sisyphus is busy working with both hands and feet. Other than that, he is a silent hero and one who is lacking in love. Yet it is love above all else that makes it possible for us to experience something more in life in the face of death. Thus it is not surprising that when people speak of Sisyphus it is usually in connection with Sisyphus *work*. And indeed, if we consider the entire train of thought connected to this work, we would have to ask in each instance: Is it a labor which we take upon ourselves because we refuse to let go of something, an idea that we can't sacrifice? Or is it a labor that is difficult, but ultimately meaningful as an experience in itself, even if we never attain the goal?

This work need not be understood as something purely external to be mastered, but as a labor on oneself. The task might be in coming to grips with a fundamental problem with which we struggle. No matter how often the same old struggle seems to be repeated it is the way in which we tackle it that brings us an increase in autonomy during the course of our lives. As long as we are firmly convinced that the problem must be overcome once and for all, we will be repelled at the prospect of taking up the stone once again. But if we can accept that our principle problems will show us only very little that is new, and that we can only achieve a certain amount each time, then we will hoist the stone when it is time to do so just to see how far we can get with it this time.

Dealing with our "boulders" then becomes a different experience. We accept that everything repeats itself. It remains the same, yet there is also something novel about it each time. It is the same stone, the same effort, and yet the way we proceed with it is new. We can gain new experiences from the process if we are open to them, and if we realize that the way to be traversed is actually the goal.

This amounts to an embracing of the rhythm of life, of the coming and going and the eternal return, and of the ongoing struggle of life and death. The movement of ocean waves is an image for this, as is sunrise and sunset. We can experience this eternal repetition as simply an "over and over again" or as an "over and over again anew." It all depends on whether or not we can come to terms with this repetition, or rather eternal return. For we can come to terms with it also in the sense that we realize that this eternal return brings something back that would otherwise be lost. In the final analysis, the issue is whether we can accept this basic law which we experience bodily, or whether we are of the opinion that it should be rejected.

An Example:
The Constantly Recurring Problem
That Changes After All

A thirty-eight-year-old man tells me that he has suffered from "inferiority feelings" his whole life. He comes from a family that felt itself rejected and inferior. In addition he was frail, and that was also held to be a sign of "inferiority" within the family. These feelings led him into therapy. The man had tried his whole life to set aside his feelings of inferiority. He had demanded a tremendous amount of himself. Yet even though he knew that he was superior to most people in almost all respects and placed more rigorous requirements on himself than others did, he still felt inferior. This "inferiority," paired with a considerable superiority feeling, is something of a stone of Sisyphus which he must repeatedly push uphill.

The therapeutic work which I began with him took the

direction of attempting together to further develop aspects of his life that were underdeveloped, so that ultimately his fundamental problem could be outgrown. This direction derives from the important statement of Jung: "In the meantime I had gained the insight that the greatest and most important life problems are basically unsolvable; . . . They can never be solved but merely outgrown." [30] Of course we cannot avoid having to deal with these fundamental problems, since they keep turning up painfully in our everyday lives.

This man's problem manifested itself in novel forms. In the early phase of therapy it appeared in his needing to be competitive with everyone and everything and then being unhappy when he was considered an "unpleasant person" that people avoided. In a later phase his competitiveness receded into the background. Instead, he devalued the achievements of other people to the extent where he gradually began to feel that he lived in a world which was worthless. All poets, composers, painters, and scientists – those who were his contemporaries – simply had nothing to say. When he became aware that he was perceiving in other people his own basic feeling, his fear that he ultimately had nothing to say himself, he forbade himself this attitude. But he could not help lapsing into it again.

In the meantime, he had come so far that he no longer needed to insist that he be the wisest and cleverest of all. In certain areas of life he had become aware of his own self-worth. And yet he suddenly began again to be competitive, to devalue others, and in the next phase to burn with envy. Again and again he struggled with these feelings, which surfaced in the therapeutic encounter.

After he gained the insight that his problem would accompany him for the rest of his life, my client became less angry when the problem reared its head to disturb him and threaten his relationships. Instead, he began to look forward with great interest to see the way in which the problem would manifest itself this time. Instead of "not that again!" he suddenly started saying: "This time I experienced my envy completely differently than in my last envy attack. This time I was not just envious, but also full of admiration for my colleague. And it was a warm admiration."

He reflected on how his problems with self-worth were showing up again in a novel way. As he noticed the look of the stone and the path it took now that he had to push again, he was reminded of all the paths that he had travelled as a result of this problem. It was not simply a repetition or a return of the same, even though to an extent that was the case. Within this repetition the man was travelling a little further on new paths.

Repetition as an Aspect of Creative Activity

The motif of resuming an effort became very clear to us in a previous example. Earlier we discussed the painter who could not succeed in painting the picture that she had seen in her mind and who kept on starting over from the beginning to create the image anew. When one looks at the series of paintings they seem to be a repetition. And yet it is clear that the articulation is constantly changing a little in the direction of a greater simplicity, which is probably what the painter was striving for.

Through repetition it becomes possible here to approach something step by step that could not be expressed in a single attempt. This seems to me to be typical for the creative process in general. Every creative person tackles again and again the ideas that have always concerned him in one way or another. In the course of his life he tries repeatedly to express what he really means or whatever it is that seeks expression through him. For many creative people, the entirety of what they have expressed in the course of their lives is in fact what they had to impart ultimately. The paths they have travelled and the footprints of their journeys are their life work, more so than a particular goal that appears to have been reached.

The myth of Sisyphus, then, represents essential aspects of the creative process, if we grant that, as with the painter, an inner image, an idea or a question forces itself upon a person and must be confronted again and again. The creative person even has the power to outwit death to a certain extent, namely in that centuries after his death his thoughts or images are still active.

Above all though, this myth presents the theme of endless repetition, which plays a major role in artistic creation. We see the creative artist's persistent concentration on his task rather than his intoxication with being godlike, though both can be associated with creativity. Sisyphus is not Prometheus.

It is the laborious aspect of artistic creation that is represented here. Here, too, we encounter the question of when to let go. The previously mentioned painter labored stubbornly and obsessively, as she herself admitted, until one day she saw another image that was more important to her to paint. She simply let the "old" picture series lie fallow. Years later she was able to paint *the* picture that had actually been in her mind all along without effort. After rolling the same stone for so long, she had simply left it lying and then taken it up again much later. For this painter taking the decision that often presents itself when this myth is translated into everyday life, namely when it is sensible to push the stone and when to let go of it, was no problem. She was open to ideas, and when another idea began to influence her more than the first one, she followed it. This openness is decisive. It gives us the chance of escaping from the compulsion to repeat.

It is clearly, then, an unalterable aspect of the creative process that we must repeatedly strive to come to grips with the content of our creation and give it a conscious form. Yet this alone is not enough to constitute creativity. In addition we must have inspiration, and that cannot be simply summoned up. Once inspired, however, our vision is brought to its most effective expression by passing through many artistic reformulations, which often include a return to the original content. Perhaps this is what artists describe as the struggle with their guardian spirit. The myth of Sisyphus expresses this, too, when we view the stone as a symbol of the god Hermes or Apollo. But even in this case the stone would have to change gradually over time and begin imperceptibly to take different paths.

In this context Goethe says:

1824, Tuesday, January 27. . .

I have always been praised as a particularly fortunate person. And I do not wish to complain or level any reproach against the course my life has taken. But in essence it has been nothing but effort and toil. I can confidently say that in my seventy-five years I have had scarcely four weeks of actual ease. It was an endless rolling of the stone that kept needing to be lifted anew. My records will make clear what I mean by this. There were too many demands on my activity, from outside as well as from within.[31]

Thus Goethe clearly indicates that the "rolling of the stone" is an issue of demand, from within as well as from without.

Once Again: Letting Go

In our discussion of the eternal return it was striking that people do not speak so much in terms of Sisyphus work when the task itself is a great strain and cannot be mastered, but rather when the endless repetition and the lack of any change becomes a torture. Endless repetition without change is abhorrent to those people who love beginnings and the emergence of something new and who each in their own way refuse to accept death. For to accept death would be to recognize endings. Death acts as a focal point bringing that which appears infinite in our lives into a rhythm of beginning and end, of onset and expiration.

People who refuse to accept death are unable to let go enough. Although they impress us by seeming to let go constantly, they are interested only in the beginnings of things and not the continuations. They hold tightly to the thought that life should be the way they wish it. They seek an eternal spring. And because they are unable to sacrifice this desire, they cannot accept the experience of repetition. They are also unwilling to discover what is new within the repetitions or to conceive of eternal repetition as the rhythm of human life which can give structure to existence. An example of this rhythm can be found in our hunger, which announces itself periodically and without fail.

When repetition is coupled with the weight of the stone which a person has to push, or assumes he has to push, the issue of letting go arises once again. We must consider whether perhaps the heroic effort of Sisyphus is being too heroically imitated, and whether because of this perhaps too little room is left over for other realms of life which are not dealt with in this myth.

After all, even Sisyphus could take a breather at least temporarily, at the point when the stone of its own accord rolls back into the valley, choosing its own path in the process. If one views the myth only in terms of failure, then the stone slipping away from Sisyphus would be labelled a "relapse." But this could also be seen as a representation of the moment in which, having given all we have, we no longer have the stone in hand, and it sets off on its own way, a way over which we no longer have any influence. It would be pretty senseless to seek control over the stone even when it is rolling down the hill. But that is just what many of us try to do.

An Example:
Relief from Duty

For a very long time some parents had cared for and protected their son and attempted to guide him in life in a way which they felt was right for him. They experienced this as meaningful work, though at times troublesome. At the age of twenty-eight the son had had enough of this loving care. He said that he felt constantly pushed and pressured by his parents. He moved to another city. Both parents were very worried that they received no more information about how his life was going. They devoted all their energy to figuring out how they could continue to supervise him without being a burden. They considered it their duty and would have felt guilty if they had devoted less thought to this problem.

It is clear here that these parents could not let go, above all because they had concentrated themselves to such an extent on their son that his life formed the central content of theirs. They were unable to let go even after he had broken away from them.

At least Sisyphus surrendered control of the stone as it rolled back down the hill. We don't know how he carried out his descent into the valley, whether he enjoyed the temporary freedom or was animated by the thought of pushing the stone again as soon as possible. In the midst of his labor this would be the moment for him to catch his breath, to breathe more easily. Sisyphus could let his shoulders fall and turn his gaze away from the stone to the landscape around him. Though the stone must always be shouldered again, there is a rhythm established between taking a breather and pushing. One can deprive oneself of this rhythm by refusing to lose sight of one's own stone and losing the ability to consider anything else.

THE MYTH IN MIDLIFE

We have proceeded from the central statement of this myth, that the necessity of death must be accepted, yet its power over life must be outwitted, in the sense that we must not give up our lives too easily to the attitude that all things must pass. It is no surprise, then, that people around forty tend to be concerned with this theme.

By the time midlife is reached it is no longer possible to deny the fact that we all must die and that life is leading us toward death. Midlife is a time in which we must bid farewell to much of what was valued before. We have either realized or failed to realize the high flying plans of our earlier years which gave our lives direction, incentive and challenge. The collision of the impossible with the possible has shown us our limits. These boundaries are not rigid. They are adjustable. In no case, however, are they infinitely adjustable, as they once seemed. We learn not only that we are allowed to be ordinary, but that we must be ordinary. The freedom and the need to be ordinary force us to say farewell to many of our ideas of greatness as well as to our exaggerated expectations of life.

Thus, while on the one hand we must constantly say good-bye to our former notions, on the other our leave-taking leads to an ever increasing degree of freedom. Taking leave of the past frees us up for new ideas, values and expectations of ourselves and others that are actually more fitting for us. Being ordinary opens up a great many ordinary possibilities in life.

The awareness that much in life repeats itself becomes increasingly frequent and widespread. So often we say to ourselves that we've seen "this" before. We recognize not only the many repetitions of everyday events, but also the recurrences of both beautiful experiences and painful ones. We then see the same events all over again in the lives of the next generation. Longings, hopes, demands and protests repeat themselves. Problems return, and the ways of coping with them are repeated. Even fashions and the tastes connected with them recur.

We must become intimately involved with the situations that are repeating themselves. If we focus only on the repetition, we will soon turn away in despair and begin to seek something completely different which is nowhere to be found.

In midlife the challenge presented by aging consists essentially of two tasks. We must learn to accept repetitions as a way of structuring the passing of time in relationship to the death which is entering our lives. But our capacity for experiencing life must not exhaust itself in merely recognizing repetition and lamenting over it. It may well be the same old stone to push, but we are capable of taking different paths with it. The great breakthrough for which we once hoped occurs, if at all, in small steps which emerge from these repetitions to permit suddenly a new experience.

In addition it becomes increasingly clear that we must take our own lives in hand if we want something to happen. We can no longer continue to attribute the guilt for what happens to someone else. We have reached an age in which we have normally attained enough freedom from parental complexes to be able to truly take responsibility for our own lives. We no longer place the burden of responsibility on our backgrounds, on our parents, or, by transference of parental complexes, on the authorities. Identifying with the best of Sisyphus, we are convinced that pushing our stone is our own responsibility and our own affair. We no longer reproach our parents for the fact that life as a whole is problematical, often painful and full of deprivation. After all, many of us have already reached the age in which our own children direct these reproaches, whether spoken or unspoken, at us.

We also realize that we are actually part of the society which we have criticized so ardently in the past. This is demonstrated by the fact that people near forty are often in positions of power in which they either participate in decision making or take the decisions themselves. Their life experience has prepared them for these decisions and they still have enough energy to carry out these decisions and the work processes that follow from them. The forty-year-olds' feeling of self-worth is no longer nurtured by the great ideas that they hope some day to realize. It is nurtured by what they have already accomplished, things which are visible and tangible.

The conscious knowledge of the fact that death is our companion makes living precious and causes us to savor the intensity in life. Awareness of death places the themes of the Sisyphus myth into a larger context with a positive sense: We try to make sure that nothing that has occurred in life has been in vain. We persevere in our concentration on whatever must be done, in a devotion to the tasks which we have chosen for ourselves. We accept the fact that our efforts will achieve something but will not move mountains.

The youthful person, however, who exists in every forty-year-old, would still like to storm the peaks. For the youth embracing the limits of human capability requires an embrace of the eternal return, acceptance of boredom and lack of productivity. This all too youthful side is embodied in the myth in the Hermes-like aspect of Sisyphus. If it cannot be sacrificed, then our feeling for life will be dominated by suffering over the fruitlessness of our efforts. Everything will seem absurd and senseless.

When Sisyphus is related exclusively to the world of work these same feelings emerge. Thus the question of the meaning of work in midlife is also important. If we keep right on pushing the stone with the youthful attitude which society expects and greatly rewards, we may wonder if that is all life has to offer. As we become more and more easily tired, we may ask ourselves in despair if this is really the meaning of life, if this is all there is.

We have here a very good question. It sharpens our awareness for everything which exists beyond the realm of Sisyphus appearing only around the edges of a life that bears the distinctly Sisyphean stamp. Included here are the cultivation of relationships, our enjoyment in relationships, the joy of existence, simply being without doing, and the recognition of longings which can take hold of us in a new way and turn our attention toward the openness of the future.

Sisyphus had to push his boulder. But we humans, even those of us who are followers of Sisyphus, can decide whether we want to keep on pushing the boulder or not. For it could be time to let go of the stone short of the peak, to renounce the experience of heroic effort which we have put forth on a daily basis, in order to take a breather and allow other aspects of being to come to life.

Even if we choose to continue pushing the stone, we have the option of approaching it with a different attitude. Instead of compulsively striving toward the goal of achieving something unique, we could choose when, in the service of which idea, and with which attitude we want to push each stone we encounter.

It may even be time to let go of the stone for good and do something different which will be meaningful to us for the remainder of our lives. Both of these are difficult choices. For even though Sisyphus can never realize his grandiose intention of pushing the rock over the mountain, his struggle remains magnificent in itself, magnificently heroic. We humans see great value in this sort of heroism, value that will outlive us if anything can.

Nevertheless, in the obsessive devotion to duty one can recognize not only heroism but also a flurry of activity which serves to blot out death and the passing of time. With this effort we try to repress the awareness that we are mortal. Our denial of death shows up especially at those times when we are reluctant to step back from an activity, because we need to keep on proving to ourselves that we can still do it. This reluctance leads to other realms of life being neglected, realms in which we could experience the intensity of life at least to the extent that is possible in our work. Finally, this reluctance to let go of the task is also due to the fact that being busy, taking action or producing an effect are values which rank very highly in our society.

The second part of the myth of Sisyphus provides those of us in midlife with an opportunity to reflect on our situation. In a society which places such a high value on achievement and the heroic fulfillment of goals, we drift all too often into the role of Sisyphus, the solitary hero.

Identifying with Sisyphus may make it easier for us to accept repetition and not shirk our obligations just because we don't experience as many new beginnings as we did when we were younger. This part of the myth may also stimulate us, no matter what we face, not to let anyone else take over for us, but to embrace our own stone and our own fate. In my opinion, shouldering one's own fate and mastering it to the best of one's ability is what constitutes the dignity of those in midlife and beyond.

Distinguishing our own responsibility from that which belongs to external forces and authorities plays an important role in midlife. Since nothing forces us to identify with Sisyphus unconditionally, we can stand back and take also a critical view of our hero. In the light of his fate we can reflect on our own situation and ask ourselves if there aren't perhaps other desires to which we could devote time and energy for the remainder of our lives.

TRADITIONAL INTERPRETATIONS
OF THE SISYPHUS MYTH

Sisyphus as Healer

In the *Dictionary of Greek and Roman Mythology* Roscher[32] attaches various interpretations to this myth. He explains that the shackling of death by Sisyphus was also an expression of the fact that he had discovered healing substances. His return from the realm of the dead could then be viewed as a recovery from a severe sickness. This perfectly feasible interpretation, suggested also by the amplification of the folk tale fails, however, to address the question of punishment. If Sisyphus was a healer, then he would seek to overcome death at any cost. If it were possible to free a person completely from death, however, it follows that he would have to shoulder his burden forever, since he would not be able to die.

Rolling the Stone:
The Work of Ocean Waves

More recently Sisyphus has been connected predominantly with the ocean, first of all directly as 'allegory of the restlessly churning tide that craftily permeates all things' or as 'the tide in its restlessly changing nature, creating and tearing down mountains, eternally industrious and artful, forcing its way down into the deepest depths and yet never failing to well up again.' His punishment in the underworld is probably nothing more than a poetic conception of the tireless labor of the ocean waves that toss themselves against the cliffs of the Isthmus of Corinth from both East and West without hope of reaching the shores. [33]

So far we have identified with this image of Sisyphus rolling the stone and have experienced the extent of the effort along with him. Now this image is replaced by the crashing waves of the ocean. What was effort – superhuman, heroic effort – before has suddenly become part of a quite natural rhythm, an expression of the energy concealed beneath the ocean, the rhythm of Life.

The concept of repetition, return and rhythm are well served by this interpretation. But when the theme of "effort" is transferred to the ocean, our identification with the hero Sisyphus ceases. For either the personality of Sisyphus would disappear when we view ourselves as similar to the waves, or we would resist identifying with this sort of heroism.

Sisyphus as Bearer of the Sun

Henry[34] views Sisyphus as a hero of the light and the stone that he pushes as the sun. He sees in the rolling uphill and downhill, the rising and setting of the sun. Of course, he imagines that the stone falls down each time on the other side of the peak, which finds no support in the text. Ranke-Graves also speaks of the stone of Sisyphus as a sun disk. He refers to a well documented Corinthian sun cult and sees in Sisyphus Helios, the god of the sun and light.[35]

In my symbolic interpretation it emerged that the stone may represent either Hermes or Apollo. The idea here that Sisyphus carries the sun across the sky can not be entirely dismissed, even though the pathway of the sun does not match the movement of the stone. The theme of rising and setting, the theme of rhythm in the sense of rising and falling remains compatible. If we consider the sun symbolically, the myth could represent man's heroic attempt to bring ever more light into his world, that is, an attempt to attain greater awareness. That, too, is a task in which we always seem to make progress, only to forfeit it again and again.

The Search for Understanding

This interpretation comes close to the one that Voelcker advocates in Roscher's *Dictionary*:

The rolling of the stone by Sisyphus can be interpreted as the hopeless striving of human intellect: Just when it believes it is about to reach its goal and soar over the pinnacle which will reveal the ultimate panorama, it sinks back down, exhausted by its futile struggling.[36]

Another interpretation characterizes humans as beings who constantly strive to transcend their limits, as Ingeborg Bachmann describes in her story, "The Thirtieth Year."

Once, when he was barely twenty years old, in the National Library of Vienna he had thought all things through to their logical conclusions and then discovered that he was indeed alive. He sprawled over the books like a drowning man and thought, while the little green lamps glowed. The other readers crept about, coughed softly and turned their pages quietly, as if they were afraid of awakening the ghosts that lived between the letters. He *thought* – if anyone truly understands what that means! He still remembers the moment when he was pursuing the problem of cognition and all

concepts lay about loose and to hand in his head. As he *thought* and *thought* and flew higher and higher as though in a swing, without dizziness, and as he gave himself the most magnificent push, he felt himself flying up against a ceiling which had to be broken through. A feeling of happiness had seized him as never before, because at this moment he was on the verge of grasping something that brought every last thing within its frame of reference. With the very next thought he would break through! Then it happened. A blow struck and shook him from within his head. A pain arose that made him stop. He decelerated his thinking, became confused and jumped down from the swing. He had over-reached his capacity to think. Or perhaps nobody could think beyond the place where he had been. Up there in his head, at the top of his skull something was clicking. It clicked frighteningly and did not stop for several seconds. He thought he had gone crazy and began to claw at his book with his hands. He let his head fall forward and closed his eyes falling into a fully conscious faint.
He was at the end of his strength.[37]

This is the human experience, to be sure. But such people grasp only the one aspect of Sisyphus, the stormer of peaks. In this case the focus is the drive for understanding, which can be linked once again to the bearing of the sun. But people like Bachmann's character lack the unwavering persistence with which Sisyphus shoulders his stone once again.

The Myth as an Expression of the Character of Coastal Peoples

Sisyphus is also viewed as a representative of the "clever coastal people, in contrast to the simplicity of the dwellers of the interior."[38] In addition Voelcker speaks of a merchant who never rests and is always traveling. And Roscher writes in conclusion:

> The results of these various interpretations of the Sisyphus myth can be summarized as follows: A recurrent natural drama, clearly observed at the double-sided beach of Corinth, namely the activity of the ocean, is concentrated here in one figure. The effect of life by the ocean is transferred to the drama of this figure. Contrary to the original sense of the myth, a single element is viewed as a punishment, for which a suitable motive is sought. This later allegorical and ethical influence on the formation of the legend is just as enthusiastically accepted by some interpreters as it is disputed by others.[39]

I could add many similar interpretations to those discussed above. I find them interesting, because all who have studied the myth have clearly chosen to emphasize individual aspects of it and have basically represented what the myth triggered in them in the way of thoughts and images. I believe that all interpretation of myths occurs in this way, my own included. All interpretations of myth are subjective, though there is some evidence to support certain views of the myth, while for others there is none. Thus one of the many reasons for studying a myth is to trigger associations that form connections between that myth and our own lives. Viewed in this way, we don't interpret the myth itself so much as our own existential experiences as they are reflected in the myth.

THE MYTH OF SISYPHUS IN A DREAM

A Summary

Mythical images still hold meaning for people today, and they continue to have an effect on our everyday lives. This is evident not only in our language in the expression Sisyphus work, but also in our dreams, where mythical images are picked up and interwoven with the personal images of individual dreamers.

Dream of a Thirty-Eight-Year-Old Woman
Nothing Can Be Torn Away From Death

The scene is a very steep mountainside. Little wagons like coal wagons are rolling down the mountain. Inside the wagons are people that look as if they are very near death. I am outraged at the lethargy of these people who are just allowing this to happen to them. I want to drag someone out of there. I even manage to get a hold of someone. I drag this person almost from the valley floor to the top of the mountain, and it is a very high mountain. Sweating profusely, I drag him to the very top the mountain. It is exhausting. In the dream I am toiling like a madwoman. I have never had such an intensive sweating dream. Sweat runs off me in streams. I don't even know whether the person I am dragging is a man or a woman. It is a naked, living corpse already belonging to death. I have the feeling, however, that if I get it up the mountain, we will be out of the wood. Up above will be life. Three times I try, and twice the person tumbles back down again. At the third attempt, when I am only two or three yards short of the peak, I have the feeling that I have succeeded, a feeling of triumph and joy. Then suddenly a giant black figure stands before me like a wall and simply throws me back into the valley. I fall backwards. I resist and wake up. At that moment I know with certainty that this is Death. The person slips out of my hands and rolls back down into the valley. I feel like I have physically been thrown backwards.

The Dreamer's Explanations

My resistance can be gauged by the fact that I seemed to have been thrown backwards from a sitting position in bed, as was reported by my partner, who was awakened by my struggling. I injured my arm, the one with which I had been defending myself against the figure. In the dream I felt myself being seized by a monstrous power. I wasn't just thrown back, I was actually smashed back by a gigantic figure that turned into a black wall. I knew with certainty in the dream: That is Death, and no one can take anything away from him. The person I had been carrying rolled back down into the valley.

These almost dead people reminded me of concentration camps and of people condemned to death. I was unbeliev-ably enraged that they refused to do anything to help them-selves. I even ran after the wagon shouting that they really must do something, and then I tore them out of the vehicle. In spite of this, two of them careened down into the valley. But the third I dragged by the sweat of my brow. And as I almost reached the top, there came suddenly this figure, and I defended myself with all my might. But Death laid me low. I was flat on my back.

The dream had a connection with my everyday world. At that time I was dealing with a suicidal patient whom I wanted to save at any cost. It was during my psychiatric residency, and I still believed that I could really have an effect, that I could motivate people. Their submissiveness towards fate outraged me: This victim attitude, just allowing themselves to be taken away! Somehow I sought to outwit death.

At the time I was extremely active and convinced that I could intervene positively in fate. This was particularly true in the case of my suicidal patient – incidentally, she's still alive. Then suddenly this dream confronted me with my human limitation, or more accurately, with the extremism of my situation. My entire superhuman protest at that time was revealed, and with one blow a limit was set to it.

After my dream, I changed quite a lot. I began to accept the submissiveness of others towards fate more easily. Before the dream I had this arrogant attitude that something could be done with these lost souls if I could just get to work on them. If one could only overcome their inertia, one could pull them away from death. Today I am much more patient in these situations. I accompany my patients, but if someone really wants to or has to go through death's door, I accept it. Naturally I still try to lead them away from death's undertow, but I no longer do so with force.

Death was a giant figure, undefined. One could see only a coat. He was cloaked and uncannily powerful, impenetrable and terrifying. He did not correspond to my vision of a gentle death. But he didn't kill me, he simply knocked me back. I found myself in the dust, and I felt like I was dust myself. I mean that in the sense of: You worm, there you are where you belong – in the dirt.

But the vivid feeling I had in the dream before Death threw me down was terrific. It was true hubris. Inside I rejoiced. I was triumphant. Even the dragging of the body up the hill was part of this: The total abandon to the task, the experience of my own potency.

This dream made me think of Camus. For him the uphill toil was almost orgiastic in meaning. I felt that too.

This dream is permeated through and through with the theme of the myth of Sisyphus. The dreamer's last thought is of Camus, and we have often considered Camus in connection with his work on Sisyphus. When I heard the dream of this colleague, who cordially offered it to me for this book, I was utterly captivated by it. I was awed by her superhuman protest and the colossal effort which she made. But I was equally frozen by this Death that set such clear limits. Although the woman had had this dream five years ago, she told it as if she had just dreamt it.

At the core of this dream seems to be the theme of defending oneself against Death and of having one's limits clearly set. For me that is also the theme at the core of the myth of Sisyphus. In her explanations about the dream, the dreamer underlines this theme by depicting it in great detail and by returning to it repeatedly, a sign of how meaningful this experience was for her.

Attempt at an Interpretation

The dreamer finds herself on a very steep mountain. To have come so far might relate to a great effort, but also to far-reaching ambition. She says that in the dream she has the feeling that if she can get this half-dead person up the mountain, they will be over the worst. Up above will be life. The expression she uses, *"über den Berg sein,"* literally to be over the mountain, means to overcome an illness or great difficulty. Mastering the difficulties in the context of the dream means being able to devote oneself to life.

The coal wagons instead of moving uphill are headed down the mountain, and they are not filled with coal but

with people who "look close to death," and seem resigned
to their fate. These people seem incapable of resisting this
downhill plunge, which parallels the rolling back of the
stone in the myth of Sisyphus. They just sit back and let it
happen. They have simply "let go." Their attitude infuriates the dreamer. She speaks of lethargy, inertia and
fatalism. But she also mentions that these people remind
her of concentration camps and of those condemned to
death. If they are condemned to death, then some power
has condemned them, and the dream-ego sets itself
against this power. The dreamer cannot accept this inertia, this giving up.

The images of these half-dead people and of the dream-
ego vividly represent the opposition between letting go
and holding on. In the dream the people in the coal
wagons simply let go. In compensation, the dream-ego
wants only to hold on and make it to the peak. Perhaps
the action of the other people should not be called "letting go," but rather "selling out" or "giving up."

The necessity of letting go versus holding on at any cost
is a theme that we considered when reflecting on the
myth. In dragging people up the mountain, the dream-
ego enters into an identification with Sisyphus, with the
difference that it believes success possible. We sense no
trace of hopelessness in the dream-ego. On the contrary,
it pitches itself with great hope against the resignation of
the others. The toiling, the breaking into a sweat is described quite vividly. But also is the feeling of completely
merging with the task, with both the devotion and the
experience of one's own potency. In a way reminiscent of
Camus' interpretation the almost "orgiastic" aspect of the
situation is stressed. The experience is not just one of toil.
There are moments of being intensely at one with oneself,
which is an awesome experience of self-realization.

The dreamer mentions only in passing that these people have twice rolled back down into the valley. It was the

dragging them up that was important, rather than the disappointment that followed. Dragging them up was so important, that in order to keep doing it the dream-ego would probably have accepted even greater failure as part of the bargain. The people in the carts are not perceived by the dreamer as having sexual identities. They are simply people who must make it up the mountain if they are to be saved. No personal relationship is involved, only a service to humanity. Though it is repeatedly stressed that these people have already been given over to death, it becomes increasingly clear that the dream-ego wants to rescue them.

The first part of the myth plays a role here: The dream-ego wants to tear away from Death what has already been turned over to him, and it approaches the task with great determination and perseverance. The third attempt is almost successful. The dream-ego is just below the peak and already beginning to rejoice. In listening to the dream, one feels the need to join the dream-ego in taking a breather.

Then suddenly the gigantic black figure rises up before her and throws her back down into the valley. This action is described in different ways. It is experienced as a feeling of being seized by a great power, which the dreamer opposes with all her resources, but against which ultimately she is powerless. She feels herself not just thrown, but smashed back, and she falls flat on her back, defeated.

The figure of Death appears in the dream as he is often depicted, cloaked, impenetrable and terrifying. The dreamer notes that he does not correspond to her image of a gentle death. It is significant in this context that he does not come in the form of her own death in the ultimate sense, but as the death of her arrogant ego, the person who aspires to the position of a god. Death demands a fundamental transformation of her attitude. This dreamer cannot spend her whole life ecstatically and orgiastically dragging half-dead people up mountains and proving to Death that she is stronger than he. Death has entered the scene for this arrogant ego, and the struggle with him is almost like the throes of death. The dreamer also senses her own vulnerability. She uses the words dust and worm, the opposites of hubris and godliness, of the triumphant feeling that can mark a human being. The black wall which the dream connects with death clearly shows that the dreamer cannot continue in this way. She must abandon her hubris. She is not killed, but one of her attitudes is.

The battle must have been intense, since the dreamer sat up in bed and struggled physically, as if it really were a matter of life or death. And it was made quite clear to her that ultimately one cannot rob Death of anything. The person she had dragged up the mountain with her rolled back down into the valley again.

In the myth of Sisyphus there is no Death on the mountain. And yet we have the impression that there, too, he is to be found in the principle that will not permit the stone to roll over the top.

The woman links this dream with a suicidal patient and with the beginning of the period in which she worked in psychiatry. Her great engagement on behalf of humanity is expressed in this dream, her power and determination. But we also see the hubris of the helper personality, the healer who declares war on death, lethargy and fatalism.

The dreamer's actions also reflect what she calls her "rebellion at that time," her protest against such suffering. If we follow this interpretation to its conclusion, the doctor who drags the half-dead people up the mountain is taking upon herself the task of correcting the injustice of creation. This hubris, which we saw earlier in Sisyphus, characterizes those very people who are possessed by the will to help others and are as yet unaware of their own

limits, the limits of human ability. Here Death comes to
clearly set those limits.

If we follow the train of thought that the dreamer
offers, we need to consider the question of whether human life should be saved at any price. Should it be saved
even if the people have chosen a different way, in this case
the way down into the valley, from where it is possible they
could walk back up later of their own accord. The dreamer says she learned something from the dream. She
learned to accompany suicidal patients, to lead them away
from death's undertow, but not by force. She learned to
accept their decision and that acceptance, though extremely difficult, is a necessary prerequisite for being able
to work at all effectively with suicidal people.

The dreamer obviously equates the half-dead people
who have lost the will to live with her suicidal patients. If
we consider them instead as images for elements of the
dreamer's own psyche, the discussion shifts. The people
in their submission to fate embody those parts of the
dreamer that let go too much, the parts that instead of
fighting simply let themselves be carried along. The
dream-ego finds these parts utterly unacceptable. Letting
go, admitting a loss or giving up don't suit the worldview
of the dream-ego. Though Death makes his presence felt
in the life and mind of this person, her dream-ego wants
to reverse the effect he has had, as though it should not be
allowed to occur. The desire to live no longer is associated
with a concentration camp, where the attitude is the
result of an extremely destructive power. It could be that
the dreamer views having to give up as the direct result of
a destructive power rather than as the natural rhythm of
life. It is no wonder then that she struggles against this
power. But this is no worldly power, it is the power of
Death. It is also conceivable that these half-dead people
embody the dreamer's own suicidal tendencies. Perhaps
she has suicidal tendencies precisely because the princi-

ple of letting go is not being allowed enough space in her life. Death comes along and makes it very clear to the dreamer that death and failure are realities. They are part of life.

This dream expresses very clearly how we can be forced to let go if we are not ready to do so of our own accord at the right moment. If we refuse to let go of things on our own, they can be taken from us.

As human beings, we do not either hold on all the time or always let go. There are some realms of life and attitudes to which we hold on too tightly and others where we let go too easily. Bringing this holding onto and letting go into the right rhythm is a question of striking a balance. Such balance is not inherent, however. We learn it by overreaching ourselves for a while and then accepting when we feel ourselves thrown back upon our human limitations. This proportion is never determined once and for all. Instead, in the course of our lives we can probably only approach it.

This is true not only of the individual but of humanity as a whole. Without our going beyond the limits, there would be no progress. And without restraint, there would be none of the responsibility which ensures that the advances made can be meaningfully applied for the good of humanity.

NOTES

Translations of titles and titles available in English, where these were obtainable, have been provided in the Bibliography. Page references in English language texts are included here in parentheses at the end of the note. All translations in this text (Bachmann, Camus, Goethe, Grimm, Jung and Kast) are my own except Lattimore's translation of The Odyssey.

1. Homer, *The Odyssey*, trans. Richmond Lattimore, New York, Harper and Row, 1968. Bk XI, l. 593.

2. *Ibid.*

3. Goethe, J. W. von, *Goethe's Werke*, Hamburg, 1963, Vol. 12, p. 516.

4. Camus, Albert, *Der Mythos von Sisyphos*, trans. H.G. Brenner & W. Rasch, Hamburg, Rowohlt, 1959, p. 100. (Engl. ed. p. 91.)

5. Camus, *op. cit.*, p. 101. (Engl. p. 91.)

6. Camus, *op. cit.*, p. 101. (Engl. p. 91.)

7. Compare Bollnow, O. F., *Neue Geborgenheit – Das Problem einer Überwindung des Existentialismus*, Stuttgart, 1979, p. 94.

8. Compare Marcel, Gabriel, "Entwurf einer Phänomenologie und einer Metaphysik der Hoffnung," 1942, in *Philosophie der Hoffnung*, München, 1964. ("Sketch of a Phenomenology and a Metaphysic of Hope," lecture given to the Scolasticat de Fourvière in Feb. 1942, reprinted in Homo Viator, Paris, Editions Montaigne, 1944.)

9. Bachmann, Ingeborg, *Gesammelte Werke*, München/Zürich, 1978, Vol. 2, p. 253. (Engl. ed. p. 171.)

10. Bachmann, *op. cit.*, p. 254. (Engl. p. 172f.)

11. Bachmann, *op. cit.*, p. 260. (Engl. p. 179.)

12. *Herderlexikon der Symbole*, Freiburg, 1978, p. 161.

13. Hunger, H. *Lexikon der griechischen und römischen Mythologie*, Reinbek bei Hamburg, 1974; Ranke-Graves, R. von, *Griechische Mythololgie*, Hamburg, 1982.

14. Compare Roscher, W. H. (ed.), *Ausführliches Lexikon der griechischen und römischen Mythologie*, Leipzig, Teubner, 1909-1915, p. 958ff.

15. Grant, Michael, & Hazel, John (eds.), *Who's Who in Classical Mythology*, London, Weidenfeld & Nicolson, 1973.

16. Compare von Ranke-Graves, *op. cit.*, p. 194.

17. Compare Hunger, *op. cit.*, p. 176ff, and von Ranke-Graves, *op. cit.*, p. 52ff.

18. Compare Plato, Phaedrus, in *The Dialogues of Plato*, trans. B. Jowett, London, 1952, p. 127f.

19. Compare Helbling, C. (ed.), *Kinder- und Hausmärchen der Gebrüder Grimm*, Zürich, no publ. year, p. 192ff. (Engl. ed. p. 209ff.)

20. Compare Kerenyi, K., *Die Mythololgie der Griechen*, München 1966, Vol. 2.

21. Compare Soupault, Re (ed.), *Französische Märchen*, Düsseldorf/Köln, 1963, p. 71ff.

22. Williams, in Kast, V., *Trauern – Phasen und Chancen des psychischen Prozesses*, Stuttgart, 1986, p. 158. (Engl. p. 139.)

23. Compare Bolte, J. & Polivka, G. *Anmerkungen zu den Kinder- und Hausmärchen der Brüder Grimm*, Olms, 1963, Vol. 1, p. 378f.

24. Helbling, *op. cit.*, p. 299ff. (Engl. ed. p. 773ff.)

25. Compare Kast, *op. cit.*

26. Camus, Albert, *Die Pest*, Hamburg, 1950, p. 60f. (Engl. ed. p. 83.)

27. *Ibid.*, p. 84f. (Engl. ed. p. 117f.)
28. *Ibid.*, p. 107. (Engl. ed. p. 148.)
29. Compare Kast, V., *Wege zur Autonomie*, Olten, 1985.
30. Jung, C.G., *Das Geheimnis der goldenen Blüte*, Zürich, 1929, p. 12. (Engl. ed. p. 89.)
31. Goethe, in Eckermann, J. P., *Gespräche mit Goethe*, Leipzig, 1948.
32. Compare Roscher, *op. cit.*, p. 967f.
33. *Ibid.*, p. 967.
34. Compare Henry (1892), in Roscher, *op. cit.*, p 967.
35. Compare von Ranke-Graves, *op. cit.*, p. 197.
36. Voelcker, in Roscher, *op. cit.*, p. 968.
37. Bachmann, Ingeborg, *Das dreißigste Jahr*, München, 1961, p. 25. (Engl. ed. p. 25f.)
38. Curtius, in Roscher, *op. cit.*, p. 968.
39. Roscher, *op. cit.*, p. 969f.

BIBLIOGRAPHY

Bachmann, Ingeborg, (The Thirtieth Year) *Das dreißigste Jahr*, München, 1961. *The Thirtieth Year*. Stories by Ingeborg Bachmann, trans. Michael Bullock, New York, Holmes & Meier, 1987. (Also contains "Undine Goes.")

Bachmann, Ingeborg, (Collected Works) *Gesammelte Werke*, ed. Koschel, C., von Weidenbaum, I., Münster, C., München/Zürich, 1978.

Bollnow, O. F., (New Security – The Problem of Overcoming Existentialism), *Neue Geborgenheit – Das Problem einer Überwindung des Existentialismus*, Stuttgart, 1979.

Bolte, J., & Polivka, G., (Commentaries on Grimm's Fairy Tales), *Anmerkungen zu den Kinder- und Hausmärchen der Brüder Grimm*, Olms, 1963, Vol. 1.

Camus, Albert, (The Myth of Sisyphus), *Der Mythos von Sisyphos*, Hamburg, 1959. *Le mythe de Sisyphe*, Paris, Librairie Gallimard, 1942. *The Myth of Sisyphus and Other Essays*, New York, Alfred A. Knopf, 1955.

Camus, Albert, (The Plague), *Die Pest*, Hamburg, 1950. *La Peste*, Paris, 1947. *The Plague*, trans. Stuart, Gilbert, New York, Alfred A. Knopf, 1948.

Eckermann, Johann P., (Conversations with Goethe), *Gespräche mit Goethe*, Leipzig, 1948. *Conversations with Goethe*, London, J. M. Dent & Sons, 1935.

Goethe, J. W. von, (Goethe's Works), *Goethes Werke*, Hamburg, 1963, Vol. 12.

Grant, Michael, & Hazel, John, *Who's Who in Classical Mythology*, London, Weidenfeld & Nicolson, 1973.

Helbling, C. (ed.) (Grimm's Fairy Tales), *Kinder- und Hausmärchen der Gebrüder Grimm*, Zürich, no year. *The Complete Grimm's Fairy Tales*, trans. Margaret Hunt & James Stern, New York, 1944.

Herder-Lexikon der Symbole, (Herder Dictionary of Symbols), Freiburg, 1978

Homer, *The Odyssey*, trans. Richmond Lattimore, New York, Harper & Row, 1968.

Hunger, H., (Dictionary of Greek and Roman Mythology), *Lexikon der griechischen und römischen Mythologie*, Reinbek bei Hamburg, 1974.

Jung, C.G., (The Secret of the Golden Flower), *Das Geheimnis der goldenen Blüte*, Zürich, 1929. *The Secret of the Golden Flower, A Chinese Book of Life*, trans. Richard Wilhelm, commentary C.G. Jung, Engl. trans. Cary F. Baynes, New York, 1975.

Kast, Verena, (Mourning – Phases and Chances of the Psychological Process), *Trauern – Phasen und Chancen des psychischen Prozesses*, Stuttgart, 1986. *A Time to Mourn, Growing Through the Grief Process*, trans. Diana Dachler & Fiona Cairns, Einsiedeln, Switzerland, Daimon Verlag, 1988.

Kast, Verena (Ways to Autonomy), *Wege zur Autonomie*, Olten, 1985.

Kerenyi, Karl, (The Mythology of the Greeks), *Die Mythologie der Griechen*, Munich, 1966, Vol. 2.

Marcel, Gabriel, (The Philosophy of Hope), *Philosophie der Hoffnung*, Munich, 1964. (French) *Homo Viator*, Paris, Editions Montaigne 1944. (English) *Homo Viator*, Introduction to a Metaphysic of Hope, tran. Emma Crawford, New York, Harper Torchbooks, 1962, also Gloucester, Massachusetts, Peter Smith, 1978.

Plato, *The Dialogues of Plato*, trans. B. Jowett, London, Encyclopaedia Britannica, 1952.

Ranke-Graves, R. von, (Greek Mythology), *Griechische Mytholo-gie*, Hamburg, 1982.

Roscher, W. H. (ed.), (Extensive Dictionary of Greek and Ro-man Mythology), *Ausführliches Lexikon der griechischen und römischen Mythologie*, Leipzig, Teubner, 1909-1915.

Soupault, R. (ed.), (French Folk Tales), *Französische Märchen*, Düsseldorf/Köln, 1963.

INDEX